见证飞虎

系列之

飞虎奇兵『鲶鱼』雷恩

Flying Tiger Extraordinaire "Catfish" Raine

Flying Tigers Witness to History

昆明市博物馆
Kunming Museum

昆明飞虎队纪念馆
Kunming Flying Tigers Museum

编

云南出版集团公司
云南人民出版社

图书在版编目（CIP）数据

见证飞虎：飞虎奇兵“鲶鱼”雷恩 / 昆明市博物馆，昆明飞虎队纪念馆编. -- 昆明：云南人民出版社，2012.12

ISBN 978-7-222-10597-3

Ⅰ. ①见… Ⅱ. ①昆… ②昆… Ⅲ. ①中美关系—抗日战争—史料 Ⅳ. ①K265.06

中国版本图书馆CIP数据核字（2012）第318763号

责任编辑：朱海涛

装帧设计：昆明凡影（原雅昌）图文艺术有限公司

责任校对：汪　涛

责任印制：洪中丽

见证飞虎

——飞虎奇兵“鲶鱼”雷恩

昆明市博物馆　昆明飞虎队纪念馆　编

出　版：云南出版集团公司　云南人民出版社

发　行：云南人民出版社

社　址：昆明市环城西路609号

网　址：http：//ynpress.yunshow.com

E-mail：rmszbs@public.km.yn.cn

开　本：889×1194 1/16

印　张：10

字　数：60千

版　次：2012年12月第1版第1次印刷

印　刷：昆明富新春彩色印务有限公司

书　号：ISBN 978-7-222-10597-3

定　价：48.00元

见证飞虎系列之

——飞虎奇兵“鲶鱼”雷恩

编 辑 委 员 会

Flying Tigers Witness to History

Flying Tiger Extraordinaire "Catfish" Raine

Editorial Committee

序一

抗日战争时期，中国曾得到世界反法西斯阵线许多国家和人民的大力援助。1941年8月1日，美籍志愿军第1大队成立，俗称为美国志愿队，由来华参战的美国志愿军组成，陈纳德上校任指挥官，协助滇缅战区对日作战。美国志愿队隶属中国空军，在缅甸完成集结和训练后，投入滇黔桂边境对日作战。1941年12月20日，美国志愿队战机响彻云霄，昆明首战告捷。云南当地的报纸新闻记载了昆明首战捷报，并将美国志愿队誉为“神鹰机队”。而此后中美新闻媒体纷纷报道志愿队英勇精神和辉煌战果时，广泛采用了“飞虎队”这一形象的赞誉，从而使得“飞虎队”的声名远播，闻名世界。从此，飞虎队捷报频传，战绩卓著，在中国家喻户晓，声名远扬。1942年7月4日，美国志愿队解散之后，美国陆军第10航空驻华空军特遣队、美国陆军第14航空队等继续协同中国军民抗战，由于这几支军队均由陈纳德指挥，因其英勇无畏和能征善战，威震长空，战绩惊人，并均采用“飞虎”图案作为队徽，以此中国的平民百姓仍沿袭“飞虎队”来赞誉他们。飞虎队与中国人民浴血奋战、同甘共苦的激情岁月，见证了中美两国人民的深厚友谊。

岁月流逝，光阴荏苒，尽管七十多年过去了，飞虎队总部所在地——春城昆明，仍然铭记着飞虎队在中国的卓越功勋。早在2009年，昆明市政府就计划筹备昆明飞虎队纪念馆，市政府张祖林市长率团到上海会晤了陈纳德将军遗孀陈香梅女士，就成立昆明飞虎队纪念馆一事达成共识。随后昆明市组成政府代表团专程赴美国拜访陈香梅女士，就纪念馆筹建工作的细节进行进一步磋商，陈香梅女士还捐赠了与飞虎队历史相关的文物资料。为此，昆明市政府特将市中心黄金地段一座民国时期的挂牌保护建筑辟为昆明飞虎队纪念馆的陈列展览场所。

与此同时，身居海外的美籍华人陈灿培先生正为他收藏的飞虎队文物寻找合适的归宿。在广州市侨联、昆明市侨联的引荐和帮助下，在得知作为飞虎队总部的昆明将建立飞虎队纪念馆，而又面临缺乏文物的窘境后，陈灿培先生立即决定向昆明市博物馆无偿捐赠其所收藏的部分飞虎队文物。

在2010年5月至2012年4月期间，美籍华人陈灿培夫妇五次向昆明市博物馆无偿捐赠二战飞虎队文物和资料。除此之外陈灿培先生还动员在美国的飞虎队老兵及其家眷也进行捐赠。短短两年时间，昆明市博物馆接受无偿捐赠的飞虎队文物资料达一千多件。这是昆明市博物馆成立至今，接受无偿捐赠文物数量最多、文物资料最为系统全面的一次。陈灿培夫妇和飞虎队老兵及家眷捐赠的文物，品类繁多，历史价值较高，其中有做工精致、质地优良的美军各式军服；有形态各异的徽章和标志；有代表二战时期的各种身份证件和身份牌；有反映二战时期政治、经济、军事的重要历史文件、实物、书籍杂志、照片信件；有战后二战老兵聚会、纪念活动的期刊、照片、纪念品、影像资料、模型等，不胜枚举。

陈灿培先生是飞虎队文物收藏的“虎痴”，更是飞虎队文物资料研究的专家。在飞虎队文物的收集、汇总、保管基础上，陈灿培先生遍访飞虎队老兵，认真核对、考究、整理文物资料的历史背景、来源、质地、用途，并为每一件文物资料编写详细的中英文注释，其认真、执着、敬业的态度让我们敬佩和感动不已。

昆明飞虎队纪念馆的成立和开馆，将进一步推动飞虎队文物的征集保管、陈列展览和宣传教育工作。飞虎队研究工作，相关学术交流活动也将迈入新的阶段。任重道远，未雨绸缪，今后我们需要做的工作还很多。首先，我们要依托现有的文物资源，进一步拓展飞虎文物征集的广度和深度；其次，我们将依托飞虎队文物资料日益丰富的优势，举办高质量的陈列展览、学术交流及纪念活动，引导更多的观众和游客了解和关注飞虎队历史；另外，我们还将加快对馆藏飞虎队文物资料的整理研究，编辑出版，为更多研究飞虎队历史的学者和专家提供方便，使昆明成为飞虎队乃至二战文化研究的重要阵地。

《见证飞虎》是专题介绍馆藏飞虎队文物资料精粹的系列丛书，其中《飞虎奇兵“鲶鱼”雷恩》是这套系列丛书中的一本。飞虎队员雷恩的文物资料，是现有飞虎队员中最完整的、最为重要的文物资料之一。雷恩的文物资料保存完好，内容涵盖了他传奇人生经历的不同时段，透过他的文物资料，我们可以看到飞虎队历史的缩影，见证飞虎雄鹰的辉煌。我们以此抛砖引玉，彰显飞虎队的历史功绩，重温中美两国人民深厚的传统友谊，展望中美两国的文化交流与合作。

编者

Preface 1

August 1st, 1941, the American Volunteer Group was formally established, led by General Claire Lee Chennault and composed of volunteer pilots; the AVG aided China in the defense against Japanese aggression in Dian-Burma Theater and was one of the most important factors in the defeat of fascism in Asia. December 20th 1941, AVG fighters score a resounding victory at the first battle of Kunming. Local and international media dubbed the group as "Flying Tiger" and the Flying Tigers have become a household name since. July 4th, 1942, the Tenth Air Force of United States Army and Fourteenth Air Force of United States succeeded the AVG after their disband and continued aiding in the war against fascism in Asia. With a winged tiger as emblem, these forces were all given the name "Flying Tiger" as a term of endearment by the Chinese people. The Flying Tigers fought courageously and achieved many victories under the brilliant command of General Chennault and alongside the Chinese people, sharing many moments of pain and joy. A strong tie of brotherhood and camaraderie was formed and helped lay the concrete foundation for Sino-American Diplomacy.

Although 70 years had passed, traces of the Flying Tigers can still be easily found throughout Kunming, where the headquarters of the Flying Tigers were located, and their meritorious still remains in the heart of every Chinese people. As early as 2009, Kunming Municipal Government was already organizing for a Memorial Museum to honor the contributions of the Flying Tigers; a meeting was held between the delegates of the municipal government and Anna Chan, the relict of General Claire Lee Chennault - commander of the Flying Tigers – in the United States where a preliminary agreement was formulated. Ultimately, the Memoriam was set up in downtown Kunming, in a heritage building, where the achievements of the Flying Tigers will be exhibited and attributed.

Coincidentally, a Chinese-American, Mr. Pedro Chan was also looking for a place to settle his collection of the Flying Tigers artifacts. With referral and assistance from the Overseas Chinese Federation of Guangzhou and Kunming, Chan was able to acknowledge the Flying Tigers Memoriam in Kunming. After learning the fact that it is in an urgent need for cultural relics, Chan immediately decided to donate part of his collection of the Flying Tigers.

During May, 2010 – April, 2012, Chan and his wife had gratuitously donated many of their World War II and Flying Tigers collection to the Memoriam in Kunming. Moreover, Chen also encouraged veterans of WWII to make additional donations. In less than two years, the Memoriam of the Flying Tigers had received more than a thousand pieces of cultural relics and historical artifacts. The number and also the scope of the donations were both more than impressive.Out of all the donated artifacts, the ones from Mr. Chan, veterans and families of the Flying Tigers were the most comprehensive and of the most historical value; these include exquisitely textured and finely preserved military uniforms; a variety of badgers and emblems; identification documents and papers from World War II; materials that clearly reflect the political, economical and social impacts of the War such as, articles, photographs, film footages, models and countless others…

Mr. Chan is a 'Tiger-fanatic', and indeed an expert in Flying Tigers heritage research. With a background in collecting, sorting and preserving historical artifacts, Chan was also able to visit many ex-Tigers veterans in order to check and ensure the authenticity of his collection. In addition he made detailed summary on the historical background, origin and purpose of the artifact in both English and Chinese. With such perseverance, dedication and passion, Chan deserves to be honorably acknowledged for his contribution to the 'Flying Tiger' Memoriam.

The opening of Kunming Flying Tigers Memoriam will further promote the collection and education of Flying Tiger's relics. The study of the Flying Tigers and the communication of information regarding historical content will also reach new heights. Despite how far we have come, there is still a long way to go in our work on the Flying Tigers. First, we must use the advantage of the myriad amounts of Flying Tigers relics to host high quality galleries and events that will draw more attention to the history of the Flying Tigers from tourists and audiences. We must also speed up the organization and investigation of Tiger's relics at hand and publish them as a resource for more scholars and experts. This will ensure that Kunming become not only a center of Flying Tiger's history, but also WWII history.

"Flying Tigers, witness to history" is Kunming Museum's pristine series of introductory collections of Flying Tigers history. "Flying Tiger extraordinaire 'Catfish' Raine is one of the books in this series. Flying Tiger pilot Raine's historical documents is one of the most complete and important collections at the Museum. Raine's historical documents and artifacts are well preserved and show cases his legendary life story. Through his documents, we are presented a unique version of Flying Tiger's history and given an opportunity to witness their glory. Carrying forward the Flying Tiger's extraordinary legacy, we can rekindle the deep Sino- American friendship and look forward to cooperation and cultural exchange between two great Nations.

Editor

序二

2007年11月，庆得广东省人民政府侨务办公室主任吴锐成先生的邀请，美国飞虎队华裔老兵及家眷有幸成团，组成回乡及捐赠飞虎文物之旅，由小弟领队，一行49人，其中11人是老兵，其余是家眷，是次共捐赠广东各博物馆共六百余件。

小弟就是从那一年开始收集美国飞虎队的文物及实物。2008年底，美国遇上金融海啸，经济不振，失业率高，中下级人民普遍感到财务有困，其间很多人也因此陆陆续续把值钱的东西在网络上变卖套现。

2009年4月小弟刚有事在中国广州，在美国的网络上看到一批飞虎飞行员遗物拍卖出售，细看之下，此乃最早期美国志愿团飞虎飞行员雷恩之遗物，心中暗喜，知是宝贝。但起标价甚高，小弟知是珍贵罕品，故亦毫无犹疑地马上出高于底价二倍落标。数日后，真是上天不负有心人，在无人竞投下，全由小弟一人独得。当时内中心情，兴奋之极，因知此批文物乃极具历史价值。

数星期后，又见有雷恩遗物在网上拍卖，吓得一跳，以为有人在制造雷恩假遗物，再次出售，追问之下，原来这件是上一手出卖时遗留下来的。再问之下，原来此人仍有多件雷恩遗物。他住在圣地亚哥（San Diego），离洛杉矶有二小时车程。于是我们约好，在圣地亚哥一餐馆见面。

是日小弟与太太同往应约，此君约60多岁，相谈之下，得悉他自11岁便开始收藏飞虎东西。因他喜欢听飞虎故事，故从小认识多名邻居飞虎队员，并成好友。年纪大后，也常到各地举办的航空展览，所以他接触到不少飞虎队员。据他说，在2005年以前，飞虎地勤人员的东西不受当地博物馆青睐，很多飞虎文物就此不翼而飞。飞虎飞行员也不一定受重视，现在可改变了，什么飞虎文物都是宝。

闲谈中，他展示了雷恩当时飞行用的皮制头盔及护目镜，并有雷恩的签名。同时亦展示一黑白相片，是雷恩当时在其飞虎战机前，戴上该头盔拍下的。相片也有雷恩的签名，在双方讨价还价中，小弟亦终以高价购入。

小弟问起他如何取得如此多雷恩之遗物？ 他对我俩说，雷恩在2005年死后，家人不知宝，尽将其遗物抛售或抛弃。他得知后，与其家人联络并一起把其遗物买走，所以能够整批保存下来。

之后在2010年，我们夫妇二人将全部雷恩之遗物无偿捐赠予昆明市博物馆。原因很简单，因二战时飞虎队的总部设于昆明，这好让此批飞虎文物在昆明得到一个好归宿。也就是今天我们能够有此福气，在此能体会飞虎飞行员雷恩的传奇人生。在此小弟也谢谢昆明市博物馆对这批飞虎文物的热心爱护，及特地出版书籍，以广传发扬。

在数年收藏过程中，不下数千余件，而最令小弟难忘及最欣慰者，莫如收购了雷恩的飞虎合约。此乃雷恩与中央飞机制造公司在华工作一年所签的原合约及签名，内书有每月工资600美元，时间为1941年8月6日。当时美军工资不外乎每月$50 - $138，而他是$600，同时还有没有写在合约内的，为提高空战士气，每打落一架日机，即获奖金 $500。以当时的生活指标，这简直是天价。但国军为扩展空中实力，再高价也得顶下去，反正都是美国出的钱。话得说过来，也因为此一合约，国军有了空战实力，取得空中优势，连挫日军节节进迫，最终胜利。可见得这一纸的合约，就是见证中国由败转胜的开始，也就是中国抗日的转折点，是极具有历史价值的。

这一纸的合约也见证了中美两国人民的友谊。中国当时正处苦难中，美国人民伸出友谊之手，提供不少人力、物资，无悔无间的助战，共同抗日。至后来珍珠港被日偷袭，美国立刻对日宣战，中美顿为盟国，联合抗战，终取得二战最后胜果。但愿中美人民的友谊永固，合作无间，发扬光大，继续创造今时今日及未来的双赢局势。

很多朋友感到奇怪，我不是飞虎队员，也不是飞虎队员的后代，为何花大量资金收藏及捐赠如此多的飞虎队文物到中美二国多座博物馆！？

首先须明白我的家庭背景。我是二战后在澳门出生的，自幼得父母的感染，对二战日军侵华时的暴行、兽行及罪行极为愤慨，故对日人全无好感。而独钟爱援华美军，尤其是飞虎队的英雄事迹，耳濡目染，从小为心目中的英雄。在半退休下，收藏英雄的文物是件开心的事，精神亦有所寄托及自娱。自己一人独享，倒不如大家一起共享。正因如此，我们的子子孙孙也有机会感受到飞虎英雄可歌可泣的事迹。这就是小弟为什么把飞虎文物捐赠予中美各地博物馆的原因，在此顺及！

我也谢谢太太，多年来花了不少她的零用钱。我的零用钱早就花光了，没有了！可幸者，我越多花她的，她越有！？真奇怪？

陳灿培

2012年10月于旧金山

pedrochan@aol.com

陈灿培

陈灿培在澳门出生，祖籍广东番禺。1967年赴美进修，有机械工程学士（1972），生物医学工程博士（1977）及加州针灸执照 #106，有12本英文著作，其中有翻译成法、葡、荷及犹太文。最新著作是每年出版的中英《全美华裔民选官员》。除关心、热心侨社外，还喜欢收藏及捐赠二战文物及华侨文物。近年来，已捐出三千多件（组）飞虎文物及千多件华侨文物与中美各地博物馆。1974年与李碧清女士结婚至今，育有一女一男及二外孙。

Preface 2

I have been an avid collector of Flying Tigers artifacts since 2007. Of the thousands of pieces I have collected, I am fortunate to have come across many of Robert “Catfish” Raine’s possessions. Raine was one of the first 100 pilots known as the American Volunteer Group (AVG) of the Chinese Air Force, or famously nicknamed the "Flying Tigers", to defend China against the Japanese invaders. I have his entire life story told through letters, pictures, certificates and artifacts. I am so blessed to have acquired Raine’s contract with the Central Aircraft Manufacturing Company Federal Inc., USA (CAMCO), which is dated August 6th, 1941. The contact was for Raine to work in China for one year, with a monthly salary of US$600.

This contract marks a significant turning point in the war against the Japanese. The AVG, later becoming the US 14th Air Force, enabled China with better air defense against enemy advances, thus paving the way for final victory.

I am glad I have found a home for these priceless artifacts at the Kunming Museum. As the Flying Tigers headquarters during the war, Kunming is the natural location for housing these items. I hope the Flying Tigers will live on in Chinese and American history and their artifacts will be visited for generations to come.

The Flying Tigers means a lot to the Chinese people. The American people offered a helping hand when China needed it the most. I hope the spirit of the Flying Tigers will stay on and that the bond and friendship between the Chinese and American people will last forever.

Lastly, I must thank my wife for allowing me to use her pocket money to fund my collection as I have spent all mine!

October, 2012
Los Angeles
pedrochan@aol.com

Pedro Chan

Pedro Chan was born and raised in Macao. In 1967, he came to the United States to attend college. He's got a BS in Mechanical Engineering (1972), a PhD in Bio-medical Engineering (1977) and a license in acupuncture in 1976. He is the author of 12 books including Chinese American Elected Officials, which has been published yearly since 2009.

He is a collector/donor of Flying Tigers and Chinese historical artifacts. In the past few years, he has donated more than 3,000 items to various museums both in China and America.

Pedro is happily married to Pek and has two children and two grandchildren.

见证飞虎

——飞虎奇兵“鲶鱼”雷恩

Flying Tigers Witness to History

Flying Tiger Extraordinaire “Catfish” Raine

目录

Contents

1

回顾飞虎 缅怀友谊

Recalling the Flying Tigers
A Commemoration of Friendship

回顾飞虎 缅怀友谊

两个强健的民族，自地球这方到那方，
走到一起，面对着面。
喧嚣和欢乐都已平息，国王和将领也已远去，
只有您的勇士啊，依然屹立。

——摘自英国著名诗人吉普林诗歌

中国人民永远尊重并怀念为维护人类尊严与世界和平作出贡献的人们。

美国“飞虎队”，一支英勇顽强，机智善战的空中奇兵，以大无畏的精神，和中国人民并肩战斗，共同抗击日本侵略者。他们响亮的名字和光辉的业绩，将作为一座永不褪色的丰碑，长存于中国人民的心中。

1937年7月7日，日本法西斯全面发动侵华战争，北平、天津、南京、上海等工商业重镇相继沦陷，东北和东南对外通道被切断。1938年8月，滇缅公路通车，日军轰炸机群开始疯狂轰炸昆明和滇缅公路沿线，企图割断中国最后一条与外界联系的通道，妄图通过正面战场的疯狂进攻和国际封锁，在“三个月内灭亡中国”，中华民族到了最危险的时候。此时，在中国云南，一个特殊的战场开辟了，一场特殊的战斗打响了。

为保护滇缅公路的运输不受或少受日军的空袭，1941年4月15日，中美达成一项秘密协议，由美国总统罗斯福签署行政命

时刻准备起飞的P-40战斗机

令，允许美国预备役军人和陆军航空队，以及海军和海军陆战队航空队的“退役人员”前往中国参加战斗。1941年7月，第一批美国志愿队在美国对日本宣战前，由陈纳德以私募的形式完成集结，悄悄从旧金山启程前往缅甸受训。8月1日，美国志愿队正式成立，总部设在昆明，陈纳德上校

停在机场的P-40战斗机

为志愿大队指挥官。从此，陈纳德将军和他的飞虎队员，与苦难的昆明和质朴的昆明人结下了不解之缘，建立并维系了长达半个多世纪的伟大友谊。

至今80岁以上的昆明老人都将永远记得惨遭日军飞机轰炸的苦难岁月。那时，由于昆明是滇缅公路的终点，也是国际援华物资转运最重要的枢纽，日军飞机不断进行空袭，市民人心惶惶。日军飞机的轰炸，使得昆明人民饱尝流离失所、家破人亡的痛苦。终于，这样的情况，随着美国志愿队的到来，得到了彻底改观。

经过陈纳德将军数月的严格训练，1941年12月20日，美国志愿队在昆明进行了第一次对日空战。日军飞行员第一次见到目露凶光、巨齿利牙、张开血盆大口迎面冲来的鲨鱼飞机，大有将自己一口咬碎的凶猛气势。此次战斗，10架日军轰炸机有3架被当场击落焚毁，飞机残骸散落在昆明以南地区。另有6架飞机在飞离中越边境途中迫降坠毁。美国志愿队以9：0的赫赫战绩，一鸣惊人。几乎所有的昆明人都目睹了这场大空战。人们欢呼雀跃，奔走相告，欢庆飞虎队的胜利。

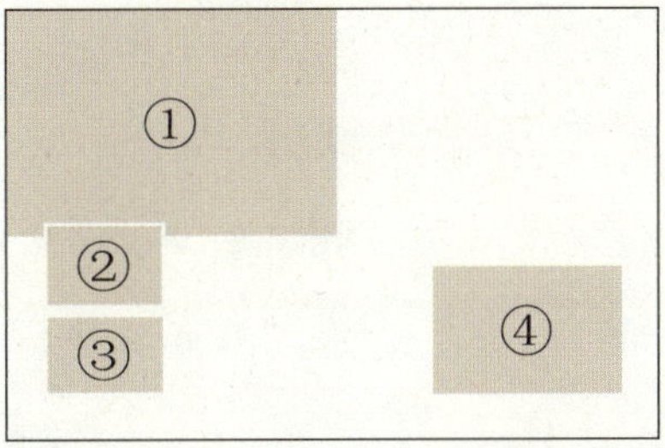

①~③涂装为鲨鱼头的P-40战斗机
④美国迪士尼设计的AVG队徽标志

美国志愿队首役、仰光保卫战大胜日寇，彻底打破日本空军不可战胜的神话，极大地鼓舞了中国军民抗战的士气。中国人

民把这支英勇善战的航空队誉为“飞虎队”。而中国的抗战，有了美国志愿队的支持，亦如猛虎添翼，必将取得最后胜利。此后不久，美国迪斯尼动画室设计的“飞虎队”队徽出炉，由一只插着翅膀的猛虎从代表胜利的V字中扑出。“飞虎”形象生动而又恰如其分，得到了志愿队员的一致认可，成了美国志愿队的队徽标志。

此后，在陈纳德将军指挥下的“美国陆军第10航空驻华空军特遣队”和“美国陆军第14航空队”也获得了这一美誉。

一次次的胜利奠定了飞虎队成为第二次世界大战中战绩最辉煌的空中奇兵，更为支援中国抗战，为世界反法西斯战争取得最终胜利作出了重大贡献。

美国援华助战空军为中国抗日战争所作出的巨大贡献和牺牲，无论中国政府还是中国人民都永远铭刻于心。对美军飞行员的无私奉献，中国人民特别是云南人民怀着感恩的心，用质朴的情意真诚回报，并用实际行动谱写了一曲曲大爱与友谊的

刚运送来的P-40战斗机

赞歌。衣不遮体、食不果腹的云南百姓，全情全力投入到飞虎队机场的修建、扩建和重建中，在短短时间里，赶建了呈贡、沾益、祥云、保山、寻甸、蒙自等10多个机场。凡是在云南境内失事的美军飞行员，都能得到当地百姓的无私救助。活着的、受伤的队员，都在老百姓的掩护下，由各级政府顺利送达昆明；死难者的遗骸也都在社会各界的关心和支持下排除万难，运返美国。时光飞渡，岁月流逝，当年的救助者与被救助者几乎都记不住彼此姓名，但他们都记住了在血与火的岁月里心灵的碰撞和真情的交融。

中美两国人民用鲜血和生命凝结成的友谊，将永远铭刻在两国人民的心中。

Recalling the Flying Tigers A Commemoration of Friendship

Oh, East is East, and West is West, and never the twain shall meet,
Till Earth and Sky stand presently at God's great Judgment Seat;
But there is neither East nor West, Border, nor Breed, nor Birth,
When two strong men stand face to face,
though they come from the ends of the earth!

Excerpt from "The Ballad of East and West"
- Rudyard Kipling

Those who contribute to the preservation of human dignity and world peace will always be respected and remembered by the Chinese people.

American "Flying Tigers"; a team of brave and tenacious warriors whose fearless endeavours changed the course of Chinese resistance history. Their unforgettable names and glorious accolades will forever be etched in heart of the Chinese people.

July 7th, 1937, Japanese fascists wage full invasion of China; Beijing, Tianjin, Nanking, Shanghai and other industrial cities fall in succession. August 1938, Burma Road opens, Japanese bombers begin rapid bombing of Kunming and Burma road in an attempt to cut off China's last remaining connection to the outside world as a part of the "three months to demolish China" plan; the nation of China faced its greatest threat during these times. It was during this period that a special battle began above the skies of Yunnan.

To protect the transportation of resources via Burma Road from Japanese bombing, America and China agreed on a secret pact on April 15th, 1941 that allowed American service men that resigned from active duty to join the Chinese people in the fight against fascism. Signed off by President Franklin D Roosevelt, the first group of American volunteers recruited by General Claire Lee Chennault headed to Burma via San Francisco in July of 1941. On

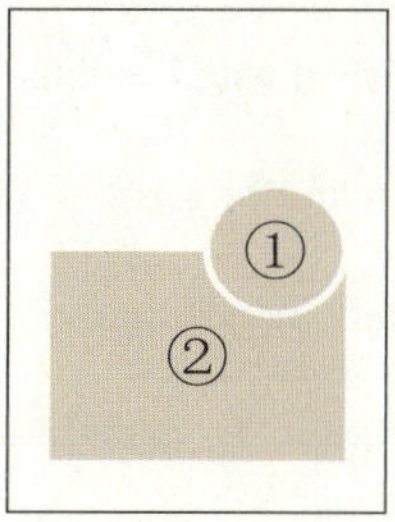

①Shark-nosed P-40 fighters

②Unpainted P-40 fighters

August 1st, the American Volunteer Group was formally established with headquarters in Kunming under the command of General Chennault. From then on, General Chennault and the Flying Tigers formed an everlasting bond and friendship with the people of Kunming that spanned more than half a century.

Elders aged eighty and up will never forget those harsh times where bomb threats had become endless and life was rendered miserable. Due to Kunming's strategic location as Burma Road's final destination, as well as an important stop in international relief transport, it was a regular target for Japanese bombers. Destruction and chaos caused by the bombings destroyed families and lives of Kunming people. It was only when help from the American Volunteer Group came that brought along change to the terrible conditions.

After months of strict training from General Chennault, the American Volunteer Group saw their first battle on December 20th, 1941.

AVG insignia on the aircraft

It was the first time Japanese pilots had been faced with vicious, blood thirsty sharks brandishing their razor sharp teeth. During the battle, six out of ten Japanese bombers were shot down on the spot and crashed south of Kunming, with another three planes crashing while attempting to reach the Chinese-Vietnam border. Final tally of battle: AVG: 9 kills and 0 losses. The spectacular victory was witnessed by almost every Kunming citizen and celebrated with cheers.

The American Volunteer Group's first battle saw the successful defense of Yangon and defeat of Japanese fleet and crushing their aura of invincibility, momentously lifting the spirits of the Chinese people and army. Yunnan newspapers referred to the AVG as "flying tigers", originating from the Chinese idiom of "like tiger with wings", describing the immense prowess and power of a tiger with wings; since then the Flying Tigers has become a household name amongst the Chinese people. Soon after the battle, a Walt Disney Studios designed "flying tigers" emblem was born; a lively, winged, tiger

P-40 fighters in assembly

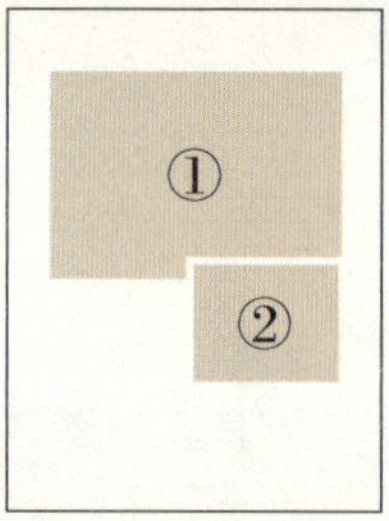

①P-40 fighters delivered to Kunming

②Women and children leveling the runway of the airport

sprouting from the letter V for victory. It was immediately chosen as the AVG emblem with unanimous consent from group members.

Later, the 10th Air Force and 14th Air Force commanded by Gen. Chennault were awarded the honor too.

Victory after victory, the Flying Tigers cemented their legacy as the most brilliant fighters in WWII and contributed tremendously to the defeat of the Japanese and end of Fascism.

The contribution and sacrifices of American pilots will never be forgotten by the Chinese people. The Chinese people and especially people of Yunnan will always be grateful of the selfless dedications displayed by these real life heroes. The people of Yunnan can only repay our heroes with rustic affections and sincere actions; constructing, expanding and rebuilding Flying Tigers airports. In a few short years, over 10 airports have been constructed in Chenggong, Xiangyun, Zhanyi, Baoshan, Xundian... Any American pilot wrecked within Yunnan boarders received the care and aid of selfless citizens. Any member, whether injured or healthy was escorted to Kunming under utmost care by citizens and government, and in the unfortunate event of fatality, the remains of the deceased were transported back to United States under the condolence and care of countless citizens. With the passing of time, rescuers and the rescued might not remember each other's names, but the connections of the soul and affection shared will never be forgotten.

No matter how high the Himalayan summits are, they can never compare to the monument casted by the blood and tears of the Flying Tigers; no matter how deep Dianchi is, it will never be as deep as the Sino-American comradery and friendship formed under the blood and fire of war.

飞虎奇兵“鲶鱼”雷恩

Flying Tiger Extraordinaire “Catfish” Raine

飞虎奇兵"鲶鱼"雷恩

雷恩的全名为罗伯特·詹姆斯·雷恩，英文名为Robert James Raine，简写为R.J.Raine。他的姓"Raine"在出生证明上错拼为"Raines"，所以很长一段时间内，他也被叫作"雷恩斯"，直到1947年他的父亲才帮他改过来。

雷恩1918年2月22日出生在美国内华达州的帕利塞兹。他从小在祖父留下的牧场中自由驰骋，追逐野马，这些经历造就了他富于挑战，勇于冒险的性格特点。雷恩在圣弗兰西斯科市立大学学习期间充分展示了他的运动天赋，拳击夺冠，热衷橄榄球。然而这些极富野性的运动也不能满足那个激情澎湃的雷恩，他向往着更为广阔的天地。1934年，雷恩服役于美国国民警卫队，1937年仅18岁的他光荣退役。1939年雷恩接受军队炮团课程的培训获得结业证书。之后，在圣马特奥民用飞行训练课程中，雷恩学会了飞行。从那时起，这个桀骜不驯的年轻人和蓝天结下了不解之缘！

1940年4月，来自内华达州的参议员皮特曼推荐雷恩进入海军航空军校学习。1940年7月，雷恩加入美国海军，成为海军飞行员，服役于彭萨科拉海军航空站。在接受严格培训后，雷恩获得在航母上飞行的资格，成为鱼雷三中队的一员，在萨拉托加号航母上驾驶鱼雷轰炸机。

在得知陈纳德招募美国志愿队（AVG）

队员后，雷恩义无反顾地选择加入美国志愿队。由于当时美国尚未对日本宣战，志愿队队员在名义上是美国联邦中央飞机制造公司的雇员。作为现役军人的雷恩也必须从美国军队中退役，以平民身份加入。于是，时任海军部航海局长的尼米兹将军为雷恩签署了从海军退役的相关文件。1941年8月雷恩与美国联邦中央飞机制造公司签订雇佣合同，以飞行员身份加入美国志愿队。1941年10月29日雷恩和其他九位飞行员乘坐“克勒普方丹”号来到缅甸仰光，开始了他飞虎奇兵传奇精彩的一生。

到达缅甸东吁机场后，雷恩立即投入到P-40型战斗机的飞行操作训练中。经过严格且近乎残酷的训练，雷恩顺利通过培训，被分派至志愿队下的第3战斗机中队，即“地狱天使”中队。

日本偷袭珍珠港，太平洋战争爆发后，第3中队队员驾驶着他们画上鲨鱼头的P-40型战斗机，前往明加拉顿机场，保卫仰光。1941年12月23日仰光保卫战打响，第3中队以3架战机坠毁和2名飞行员牺牲换来了击落日机25架的骄人战绩，这是空战史上以少胜多的典型战例，这也是雷恩所在的第3中队送

走出机舱的雷恩

①飞行中的B-24轰炸机

②英姿飒爽的雷恩戎装像

给飞虎将军陈纳德最好的圣诞礼物。这期间雷恩并没有参加第3中队的战斗，他忙于运送在非洲的P-40战斗机。1942年4月起，雷恩正式投入到战斗中，在萨尔温江峡谷（怒江峡谷）战役中，雷恩和六名飞行员就阻止了日军的前进。23岁的雷恩有幸成为飞虎队中最年轻、最英勇的队员之一。雷恩有个绰号，即“Catfish”，翻译成中文是“鲶鱼”之意，得名典故无从考证，但从鲶鱼浑身滑溜溜，很难被敌人捕获这一特性上考虑，“鲶鱼”和飞行技艺高超，常常从敌人眼皮下溜走的雷恩确实很有几分相像。

1942年7月4日，美国志愿队解散。这时的雷恩已经成为第3中队的主攻飞行员、分队长，有击落3.2架日机的辉煌战绩。在飞虎陈纳德将军亲笔签署的文件中，雷恩和另外19个飞行员荣升为飞行领航员。

因为在援华抗战中的英勇贡献，雷恩获得由国民政府主席林森颁发勋章证书，六等云麾勋章。在飞虎将军陈纳德亲笔签名的信件中，也告知雷恩其获得国民政府颁发的六等云麾勋章和三星翼章。

美国志愿队解散后，雷恩自愿留下参与培训美军第23战斗机大队（即美国空军驻华特遣队，隶属美军第10航空队）的飞行员驾驶P-40战斗机。在两周的培训任务结束后，雷恩跟随美军第23战斗机大队来到印度进行短暂休整。

1942年8月，爱好飞行的雷恩和其他的10余位志愿队员一同加入了中国航空公司（CNAC），因为在这里，他们这些身经百战的飞行员，又将面临着新的飞行挑战，那就是驾驶着满载作战物资和人员的运输机挑战飞行极限，飞越“世界屋脊”喜马拉雅山脉。这条航线途径气候恶劣的雪山峡谷、人迹罕至的原始森林，飞行过程中还要提防日军飞机的拦截，被称为驼峰航线或死亡航线。截止到1945年3月，雷恩驾驶运输机飞行在这条死亡航线上，往返于印度和昆明之间，共完成了443次飞越驼峰的运输任务。然而富于挑战的雷恩不甘于终日穿梭在驼峰航线上运输人员和物资，他为没有机会和敌机相遇而沮丧。在二战将结束的最后时刻，他加入美国海军，重返战场，驾驶战斗机进攻日本本土。

二战结束后，雷恩与另外几位飞行员以原始股东身份在美组建飞虎航空公司（原名为全国天空货运公司）。

经过几年的发展，飞虎航空公司已成为当时全球最大的航空货运公司。雷恩选择担任机长，继续飞行。雷恩一生飞行生涯中飞行记录超过32000小时，驾驶过各式各样的飞机，如螺旋桨驱动的海军培训机、P-40战斗机、喷气式运输机等。

1978年，雷恩从航空公司退休。退休后的雷恩回到了故乡内华达州，重拾对牧场的热爱，他驯养名种赛马进行比赛，再一次将自己的爱好发展成为人生中的另一项成就。

战后，雷恩多次参加志愿队和中国航空公司的聚会活动。2001年雷恩和部分飞虎队老兵应邀，回到昆明，故地重游，受到春城昆明市民的热情接待。

2005年3月25日，和病魔顽强抗争了很长时间的“鲶鱼”雷恩在内华达州里诺市圣玛丽医院逝世，但他顽强、勇敢、执着、乐观的形象已永远被我们所铭记。

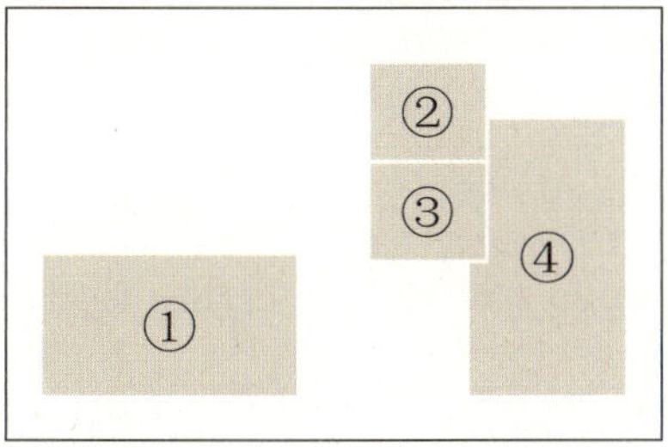

①、②停在机场的双翼教练机

③准备起飞的P-40战斗机

④身穿海军军服的雷恩

Flying Tiger Extraordinaire "Catfish" Raine

Robert James. "Catfish" Raine was born on Febuary 22nd, 1918, in Palisades, Nevada. Often known as "Raines" due to a registration error on his birth certificate. He spent much of his childhood on his father's ranch in Pine Valley, Nevada and graduated from Reno High school in 1939. He was more at home chasing horses than he was in the classroom. Raine attended San Francisco City College where he boxed, winning one title and played football. He entered the United States Navy in July, 1940 appointed to Pensacola Naval Officers Training Program and gained his carrier status aboard the USS Saratoga and was assigned to Torpedo Squadron 3. In 1941 Raine was recruited by the American Volunteer Group (AVG) "The Flying Tigers" commanded by Claire Lee Chenault as a civilian to aid the Chinese Air Force against the Japanese Empire. In mid 1941, he set sail on the ship "Klipfontein" with 9 other pilots, arriving in Rangoon Burma on October

29th, 1941 and was assigned the 3rd Pursuit Squadron “Hell’s Angels” flying P-40 fighters and began the most exciting chapter of his flying career.

On December 23rd 1941, after the Japanese invasion of Pearl Harbor, the 3rd Squadron achieved combat victories over 25 Japanese fighters with the sacrifice of 3 of their own planes and 2 pilots. The victory cemented the AVG as elite pilots and also earned them the nickname of “The Flying Tigers” amongst Yunnan locals. Raine was not present at this battle as he was busy transporting P-40s in Africa. In April 1942 at the battle of Salween Gorge, Raine and 6 other pilots single handedly stopped the entire Japanese Army’s advances. As a Flight Leader in the 3rd Pursuit Squadron, he was credited with 3.20 air-to-air victories.

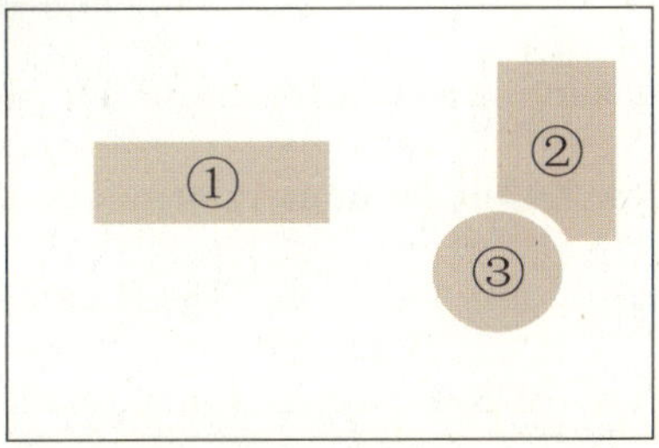

①Raine and his instructor in the trainer

②Raine with his relative

③Raine and his friend

Nicknamed "Catfish" for his superb flying skills and slippery nature in battles, for his WWII services, Raine earned 2 Distinguished Flying Crosses, Order of Resplendent Banner with Special Rosette, 3 Star Wings, Air Medal and Medal Certificate from Nationalist Government Chairman Linsen.

After the AVG disbanded, Raine was one of the AVG pilots who volunteered to stay an extra two weeks to help train incoming American United States Army Air Force (USAAF) pilots for the newly formed 23rd Fighter Group, flying P-40s . After his brief tour with the 23rd FG, Mr. Raine, along with seventeen other Flying Tigers, joined the China National Aviation Corporation (CNAC), flying supplies between India and China. He flew 443 hazardous missions over the Himalayas, also known as "The Hump", until March of 1945. Between then and the end of the war, Raine enlisted in the Navy. After the war, he returned to the United States and was one of ten original investors who organized the Flying Tiger Lines, which in time became the country's largest air freight carrier. In 1947 he followed Chennault to Shanghai joining Civil Air Transport as a cargo pilot. Returning to the US in the 50's He stayed with the operational side of the airline, becoming a captain and one of the company's most senior pilots. Raine logged more than 32,000 hours of flight time during his career, from propeller driven Navy trainers to jet powered transports. He retired from the airline in 1978, and once again calls Nevada his home, where he has raised champion racing horses for many years.

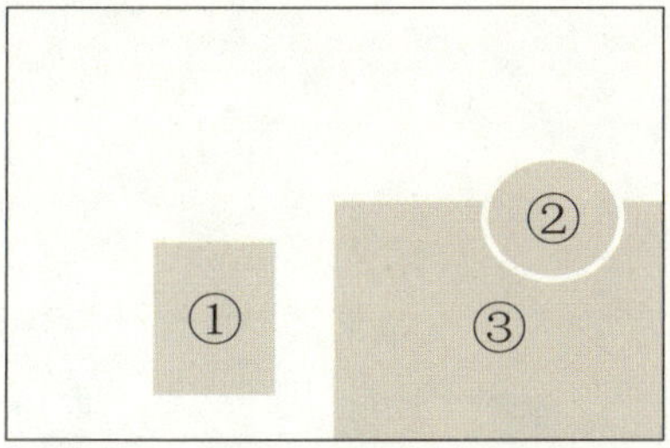

①Raine in the US navy uniform

②A biplane trainer

③P-40 fighters in shipment

108

3

奇兵遗珍 见证往事

Extraordinaire Legacy
Witness to History

奇兵遗珍　见证往事

飞虎奇兵雷恩的私人物品中有证件、文件、书信、协议、收入清单、人寿保险和实物等。虽然零星的文物不能完整地展示雷恩的人生轨迹，但这已经是我们所能见到的个人资料最为丰富的一位，其中的大部分文物资料涉及二战飞虎队历史相关内容，是见证飞虎队历史的珍贵物证。这些历史文物，就像一颗颗散落的珍珠，以点带面，穿缀成串，引导我们回到二战时期的烽火岁月……

遥想当年，在战火纷飞的年代，曾经有多少踌躇满志的美国年轻人，他们风华正茂，激情满怀，不远万里来到中国，和中国人民一起浴血奋战，抗击日寇。他们都是在二战中立下赫赫战功的英雄，其中有不少人甚至献出了年轻宝贵的生命。这些英雄，都应当彪炳史册，接受后人的纪念、缅怀和景仰。可漫长的历史，正在无情地湮没他们，他们的理想抱负，他们的音容笑貌，言行举止，他们参加飞虎队前后的人生经历，变成一个个历史谜团，让我们十分惋惜。幸好雷恩留下的这些文物资料，让我们了解雷恩的同时，也能透过层层迷雾，揭开历史神秘的面纱，使飞虎队英雄们的光辉形象在后人面前日益清晰、鲜活起来。

现在，让我们透过一件件尘封多年的文物资料，一起走近当年的飞虎奇兵“鲶鱼”雷恩。

历史回到70多年前——也许，雷恩正徜徉在昆明街头享受着和煦的阳光；或许，他正在晴朗的蓝天白云间驾机翱翔，追踪和阻击日军的飞机……

Extraordinaire Legacy Witness to History

Flying Tiger extraordinaire Raine’s personal artifacts includes certificates, documents, letters, contracts, bank statements, insurance policies and more. Although scattered artifacts can’t completely portray an Raine’s life story, they are essential to understanding his history and testifying the legacy of WWII and the Flying Tigers. The collection of personal artifacts is one of the most complete in modern history and our greatest guide to life during WWII.

What is a hero? A hero is someone who works beyond the scopes of what they are asked, someone who reacts in the moment to social needs and injustices; putting the wellbeing of others above their own, even at the price of their own life. War-torn times saw countless compassionate, complacent young Americans traveling to China to fight Japanese imperialism side by side with the Chinese people. They are the nameless heroes whose services will be forever etched in history and inspire generations to come. But time is merciless, over the course of decades time has been annihilating the memories of these heroes; their dreams and ambitions, their smiles and voices, their demeanors and their life story. We cannot let their stories be forgotten and become a mystery of time. The artifacts Raine left us allows us to transcend the mist of time and bring to life the personas of these heroes for the world to see.

Let us walk into the life of "Catfish" Raine through the portal of historical documents. History returns to 1940's ——maybe Raine is sitting in the streets of Kunming enjoying the radiance of the sun; or maybe he's soaring through the skies, tracking and tangling with enemy fighters...

雷恩的美国国民警卫队退役证明

Letter of honorable discharge and enlistment record

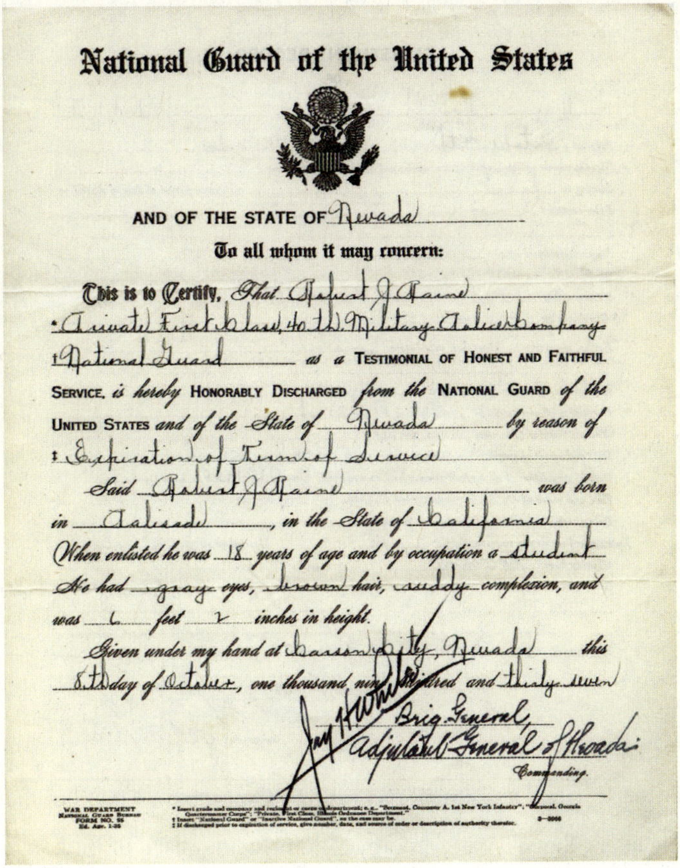

National Guard of the United States

AND OF THE STATE OF Nevada

To all whom it may concern:

This is to Certify, That Robert J Raine
Private First Class, 40th Military Police Company
National Guard as a TESTIMONIAL OF HONEST AND FAITHFUL SERVICE, is hereby HONORABLY DISCHARGED from the NATIONAL GUARD of the UNITED STATES and of the State of Nevada by reason of
Expiration of Term of Service

Said Robert J Raine was born in Palisade, in the State of California

When enlisted he was 18 years of age and by occupation a student

He had gray eyes, brown hair, ruddy complexion, and was 6 feet 2 inches in height.

Given under my hand at Carson City, Nevada this 8th day of October, one thousand nine hundred and thirty seven

Jay H White
Brig. General,
Adjutant General of Nevada
Commanding.

WAR DEPARTMENT
NATIONAL GUARD BUREAU
FORM NO. 56

1937年10月8日签发的美国国民警卫队退役证明。其中记录了雷恩入役时间为1934年10月9日，国民警卫队退役时年仅18岁。证明中各种相关信息条目内容较多，记录翔实，比如雷恩出生地为美国内华达州的帕利塞兹，他的体貌特征等基本情况记载得很详细。

【背景知识】：美国国民警卫队（National Guard of the United States），常简称为国民兵，是美国军队一支美国预备役军事部队，由各州国民警卫队单位组成，不论是否现役，均受联邦政府认可。士兵皆为民兵，平常从事各行各业，旗下一分为二，有陆军国民警卫队及空军国民警卫队。

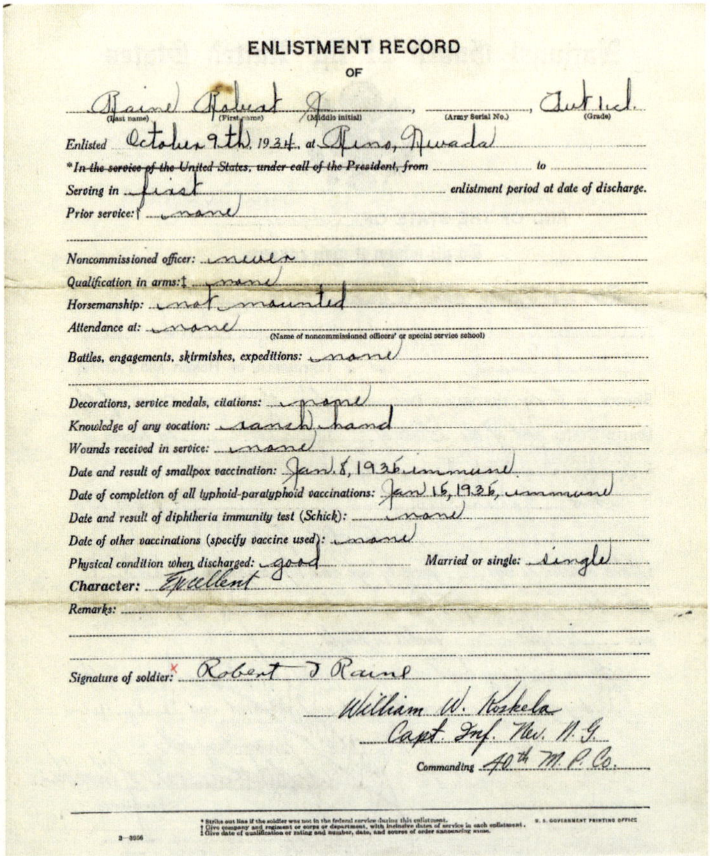

ENLISTMENT RECORD

OF

Raine Robert J., ______ (Army Serial No.), Pvt 1cl. (Grade)
(Last name) (First name) (Middle initial)

Enlisted October 9th, 1934, at Reno, Nevada

~~*In the service of the United States, under call of the President, from~~ ______ to ______

Serving in first enlistment period at date of discharge.

Prior service:† none

Noncommissioned officer: never

Qualification in arms:‡ none

Horsemanship: not mounted

Attendance at: none
(Name of noncommissioned officers' or special service school)

Battles, engagements, skirmishes, expeditions: none

Decorations, service medals, citations: none

Knowledge of any vocation: ranch hand

Wounds received in service: none

Date and result of smallpox vaccination: Jan. 8, 1936 immune

Date of completion of all typhoid-paratyphoid vaccinations: Jan 16, 1936, immune

Date and result of diphtheria immunity test (Schick): none

Date of other vaccinations (specify vaccine used): none

Physical condition when discharged: good Married or single: single

Character: Excellent

Remarks:

Signature of soldier: Robert J Raine

William W. Koskela
Capt. Inf. Nev. N.G.
Commanding 40th M.P. Co.

* Strike out line if the soldier was not in the federal service during this enlistment.
† Give company and regiment or corps or department, with inclusive dates of service in each enlistment.
‡ Give date of qualification or rating and number, date, and source of order announcing same.

3—3906

U. S. GOVERNMENT PRINTING OFFICE

Letter of honorable discharge and enlistment record from the National Guard of the United States. The enlistment record contained Raine's basic information including place of birth, age of enrollment and his physical traits. Raine was honorably discharged by reason of expiration of terms of service.

Background:The National Guard was established as a federally funded reserve component of the nation's armed forces on January 21st 1903. The National Defense Act of 1947 created the Air Force as a separate branch of the Armed Forces of the United States and concurrently created the Air National Guard as one of its reserve components, mirroring the Army's component structure. The National Guard of the several states, territories and the District of Columbia serves as part of the first-line defense for the United States. The state National Guard is organized into units stationed in each of the 50 states and US territories, and operates under their respective state governor or territorial adjutant general.

1940年9月30日，位于美国福罗里达州彭萨克拉的美国海军航空站受训人员152C名单中，53名飞行受训人员按名字的字母顺序，被分为左右两队。雷恩位列右队。编组旨在进行地面和飞行交替训练。在现有的文物资料中，正是从这一份文件开始，雷恩的名字错写为Raines.Robert.J 即“雷恩斯”。从此以后直到1947年，雷恩的名字始终错拼为“雷恩斯”。

Starting from this list, the name of Raine, Robert J. had been misspelled to Raines, Robert J. This was not corrected until 1947.

雷恩四枚徽章
Miscellaneous pins

四枚徽章金属质地，形态各异，各具特色，是雷恩加入AVG前的徽章。

Metal texture, various shapes and distinctive features.Origin unknown.

雷恩的购车发票

Invoice from car dealer

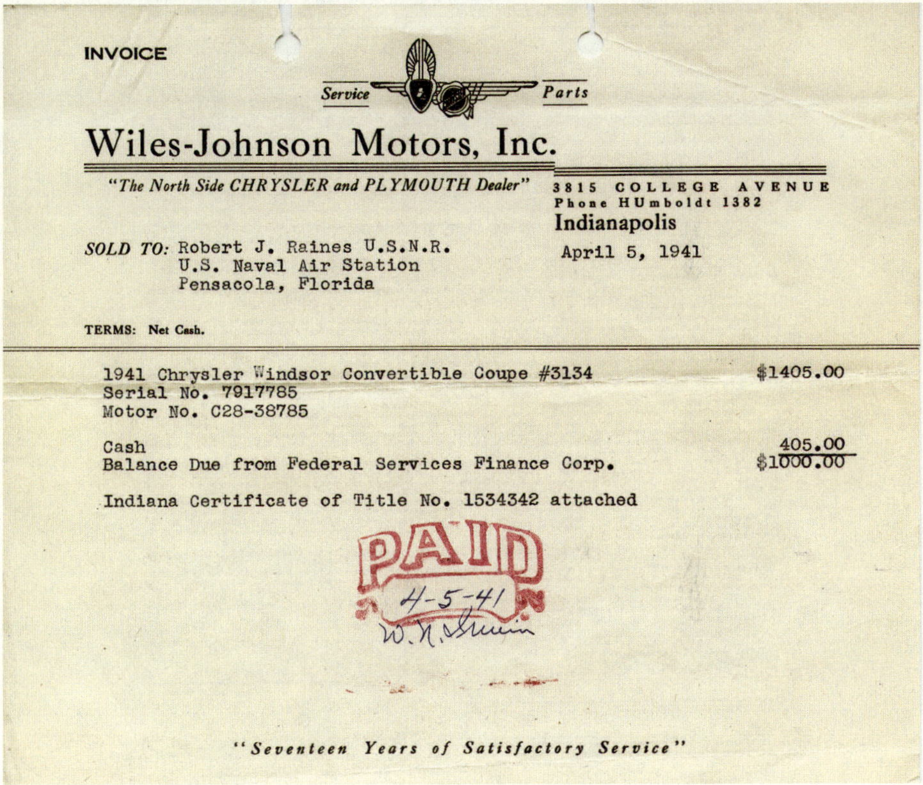
INVOICE

Service Parts

Wiles-Johnson Motors, Inc.

"The North Side CHRYSLER and PLYMOUTH Dealer"

3815 COLLEGE AVENUE
Phone HUmboldt 1382
Indianapolis

SOLD TO: Robert J. Raines U.S.N.R.
U.S. Naval Air Station
Pensacola, Florida

April 5, 1941

TERMS: Net Cash.

1941 Chrysler Windsor Convertible Coupe #3134	$1405.00
Serial No. 7917785	
Motor No. C28-38785	
Cash	405.00
Balance Due from Federal Services Finance Corp.	$1000.00

Indiana Certificate of Title No. 1534342 attached

PAID
4-5-41
W. N. [illegible]

"Seventeen Years of Satisfactory Service"

Invoice from car dealer. Raine bought a 1941 Chrysler Windsor Convertible Coupe on Feb 5th 1941.

1941年4月5日雷恩的购车发票，显示购车人雷恩是美国福罗里达州彭萨克拉的美国海军航空站成员 。从发票中可以了解到雷恩购买了克莱斯勒—温莎敞篷跑车，车型为3134型，发动机号C28−38785；车价为1405美元。在发票中还有销售公司“满意服务17年”的售后服务承诺字样。

抵押贷款合同

Mortgage agreement

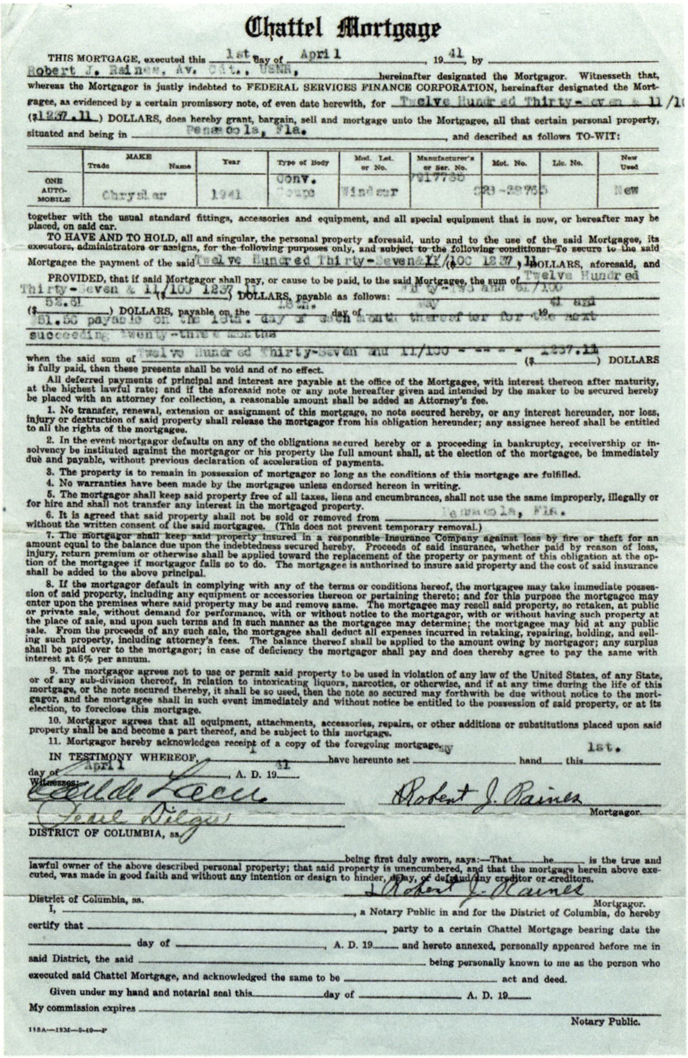

Chattel Mortgage

THIS MORTGAGE, executed this 1st day of April, 1941, by Robert J. Rainey, Av. Cdt., USNR, hereinafter designated the Mortgagor. Witnesseth that, whereas the Mortgagor is justly indebted to FEDERAL SERVICES FINANCE CORPORATION, hereinafter designated the Mortgagee, as evidenced by a certain promissory note, of even date herewith, for Twelve Hundred Thirty-Seven & 11/100 ($1237.11) DOLLARS, does hereby grant, bargain, sell and mortgage unto the Mortgagee, all that certain personal property, situated and being in Pensacola, Fla., and described as follows TO-WIT:

	MAKE Trade	Name	Year	Type of Body	Mod. Let. or No.	Manufacturer's or Ser. No.	Mot. No.	Lic. No.	New Used
ONE AUTO-MOBILE	Chrysler		1941	Conv. Coupe	Windsor	7917780	C28-28765		New

together with the usual standard fittings, accessories and equipment, and all special equipment that is now, or hereafter may be placed, on said car.

TO HAVE AND TO HOLD, all and singular, the personal property aforesaid, unto and to the use of the said Mortgagee, its executors, administrators or assigns, for the following purposes only, and subject to the following conditions: To secure to the said Mortgagee the payment of the said Twelve Hundred Thirty-Seven & 11/100 ($1237.11) DOLLARS, aforesaid, and

PROVIDED, that if said Mortgagor shall pay, or cause to be paid, to the said Mortgagee, the sum of Twelve Hundred Thirty-Seven & 11/100 ($1237.11) DOLLARS, payable as follows: Fifty-Two and 61/100 ($52.61) DOLLARS, payable on the 18th day of May, 1941 and $51.50 payable on the 18th. day of each month thereafter for the next succeeding twenty-three months

when the said sum of Twelve Hundred Thirty-Seven and 11/100 - - - - - ($1237.11) DOLLARS is fully paid, then these presents shall be void and of no effect.

All deferred payments of principal and interest are payable at the office of the Mortgagee, with interest thereon after maturity, at the highest lawful rate; and if the aforesaid note or any note hereafter given and intended by the maker to be secured hereby be placed with an attorney for collection, a reasonable amount shall be added as Attorney's fee.

1. No transfer, renewal, extension or assignment of this mortgage, no note secured hereby, or any interest hereunder, nor loss, injury or destruction of said property shall release the mortgagor from his obligation hereunder; any assignee hereof shall be entitled to all the rights of the mortgagee.

2. In the event mortgagor defaults on any of the obligations secured hereby or a proceeding in bankruptcy, receivership or insolvency be instituted against the mortgagor or his property the full amount shall, at the election of the mortgagee, be immediately due and payable, without previous declaration of acceleration of payments.

3. The property is to remain in possession of mortgagor so long as the conditions of this mortgage are fulfilled.

4. No warranties have been made by the mortgagee unless endorsed hereon in writing.

5. The mortgagor shall keep said property free of all taxes, liens and encumbrances, shall not use the same improperly, illegally or for hire and shall not transfer any interest in the mortgaged property.

6. It is agreed that said property shall not be sold or removed from Pensacola, Fla. without the written consent of the said mortgagee. (This does not prevent temporary removal.)

7. The mortgagor shall keep said property insured in a responsible Insurance Company against loss by fire or theft for an amount equal to the balance due upon the indebtedness secured hereby. Proceeds of said insurance, whether paid by reason of loss, injury, return premium or otherwise shall be applied toward the replacement of the property or payment of this obligation at the option of the mortgagee if mortgagor fails so to do. The mortgagee is authorized to insure said property and the cost of said insurance shall be added to the above principal.

8. If the mortgagor default in complying with any of the terms or conditions hereof, the mortgagee may take immediate possession of said property, including any equipment or accessories thereon or pertaining thereto; and for this purpose the mortgagee may enter upon the premises where said property may be and remove same. The mortgagee may resell said property, so retaken, at public or private sale, without demand for performance, with or without notice to the mortgagor, with or without having such property at the place of sale, and upon such terms and in such manner as the mortgagee may determine; the mortgagee may bid at any public sale. From the proceeds of any such sale, the mortgagee shall deduct all expenses incurred in retaking, repairing, holding, and selling such property, including attorney's fees. The balance thereof shall be applied to the amount owing by mortgagor; any surplus shall be paid over to the mortgagor; in case of deficiency the mortgagor shall pay and does thereby agree to pay the same with interest at 6% per annum.

9. The mortgagor agrees not to use or permit said property to be used in violation of any law of the United States, of any State, or of any sub-division thereof, in relation to intoxicating liquors, narcotics, or otherwise, and if at any time during the life of this mortgage, or the note secured thereby, it shall be so used, then the note so secured may forthwith be due without notice to the mortgagor, and the mortgagee shall in such event immediately and without notice be entitled to the possession of said property, or at its election, to foreclose this mortgage.

10. Mortgagor agrees that all equipment, attachments, accessories, repairs, or other additions or substitutions placed upon said property shall be and become a part thereof, and be subject to this mortgage.

11. Mortgagor hereby acknowledges receipt of a copy of the foregoing mortgage.

IN TESTIMONY WHEREOF, I have hereunto set my hand this 1st. day of April, A. D. 1941

Witnesses: Claude Lacy

Pearl Dilger

Robert J. Rainey, Mortgagor.

DISTRICT OF COLUMBIA, ss.

______ being first duly sworn, says:—That he is the true and lawful owner of the above described personal property; that said property is unencumbered, and that the mortgage herein above executed, was made in good faith and without any intention or design to hinder, delay, or defraud any creditor or creditors.

Robert J. Rainey, Mortgagor.

District of Columbia, ss.

I, ______, a Notary Public in and for the District of Columbia, do hereby certify that ______, party to a certain Chattel Mortgage bearing date the ______ day of ______, A. D. 19__ and hereto annexed, personally appeared before me in said District, the said ______ being personally known to me as the person who executed said Chattel Mortgage, and acknowledged the same to be ______ act and deed.

Given under my hand and notarial seal this ______ day of ______ A. D. 19__

My commission expires ______

Notary Public.

115A—15M—5-40—P

1941年4月1日，雷恩与联邦金融服务公司签署了贷款合同。他贷款1237.11美元，用于购买克莱斯勒—温莎敞篷车。贷款执行期限23个月，每月18日为还款日，每月还款金额为51.5美元。

Raine signed a mortgage agreement on April 1st 1941.

雷恩海军飞行员证书

Naval Aviator Certificate with Raine's ID photo

1941年5月21日颁发给雷恩的海军飞行员证书，由美国海军部航海局长尼米兹（后为美国海军五星上将、太平洋舰队总司令）于1941年5月7日亲笔签署。证件编号为7613号。证件显示雷恩出生于1918年2月18日。证件中有一张雷恩的半身证件黑白照片，雷恩风华正茂，英姿飒爽。照片下侧盖有发证机关美国海军部的钢印。

Naval Aviator Certificate with Raine's ID photo.

海军飞行员金色徽章
Naval Aviation Observer (Navigation) badge

徽章呈金色，金属质地，形似展开的飞机双翼，造型别致，气韵非凡。

Golden color, metal texture, shape like spread-wings.

海军飞行员金丝徽章

Triangular Coils Bullion Wings Badge

徽章略呈三角形，深绿色布地，上绣金丝线飞翼展翅。构思奇巧，端庄大方。

Triangular, bottle green color, cloth texture, spread wings embroidered in golden thread, elaborate design.

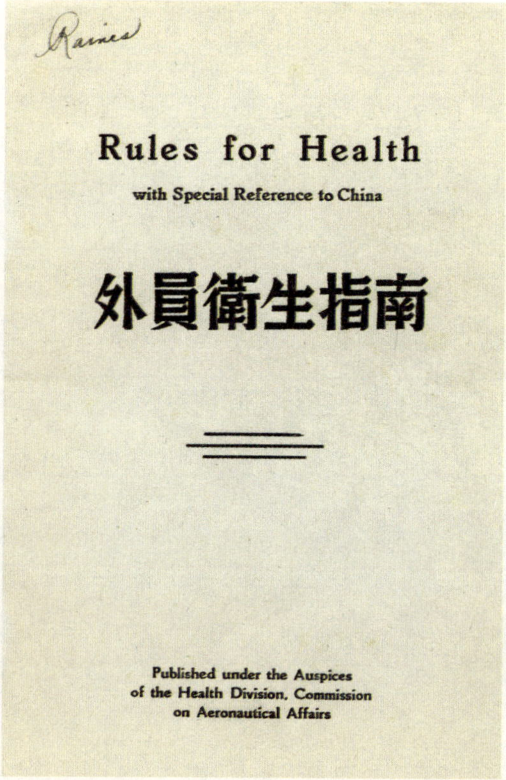

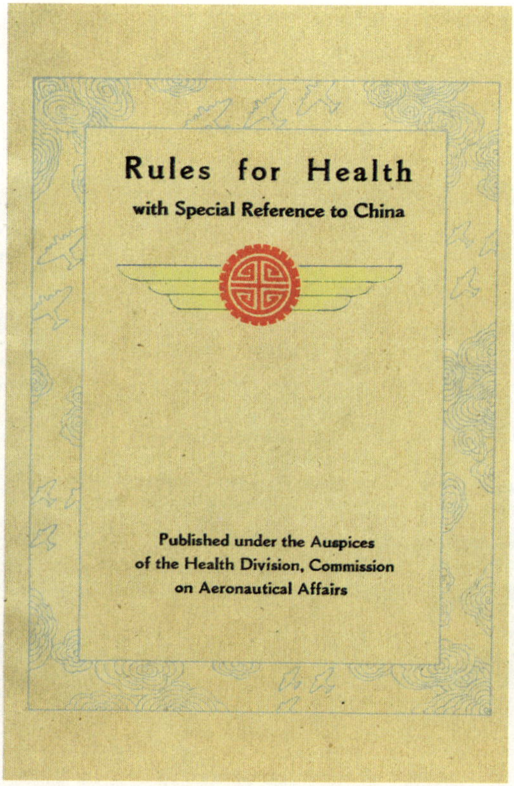

该指南1941年7月28日由空军事务委员会健康部赞助出版，英文版，内有18页。手册左上角上有雷恩钢笔签名。书中扉页内有孙中山、蒋介石的照片以及中国空军旗帜等图片。手册内容针对外援在华的卫生和健康等问题提出了建设性的意见和指导。

Flag of the Chinese Air Force

Health and Victory

Raine's signature is on the cover's left corner. Total is 18 pages. The images of Soong Tse-ven, Chiang Kai-shek and Chinese Air Force flag are on the front page.

The booklet was published under the auspices of the Health Division, Commission on Aeronautical Affairs on July 28th, 1941.

雷恩与中央飞机制造公司签订的合同

The contract of employment signed by Raine and the Central Aircraft Manufacturing Company (CAMCO)

雷恩参加美国志愿队的合同签订于1941年8月6日，签约地点为圣地亚哥。由于当时美日尚未宣战，志愿队员是以平民身份参战，因此与志愿队员签约的公司是美国联邦中央飞机制造公司。在合同中，签约双方约定条款详尽，对工资待遇、出发时间、差旅费用、假期、保险福利等各方面都有详尽的约定。比如每月支付给雷恩的工资是600美元，并于每个月最后一天发放；要求雷恩的报到日期不得晚于1941年8月28日；在合同的最后，有雷恩的亲笔签名。

Raine signed the contract to join the American Volunteer Group on August 6th, 1941 in San Diego. The United States has not yet declared war on Japan; the American Volunteer Group participated in the war under civilian identity. As a result, the U.S. Federal Central Aircraft Manufacturing Company signed the contract on behalf of the AVG.

【背景知识】：1940年底，陈纳德和航空委员会委员毛邦初到美国，谋求得到作战飞机并招募飞行人员。几经周折，1941年3月11日，罗斯福总统签署了“租借法案”，按照这项法案，战斗机等武器装备可以作为租借物资出租给中国或其他国家。同年4月15日罗斯福总统又签署了一项密令，允许美国陆、海军退役军人及预备役军人参加美国志愿队前往中国。美国政府向中国提供了的100架P-40B战斗机。陈纳德与蒋介石的私人代表宋子文以“中央飞机制造公司”的名义在美国各地招募飞行员地勤人员，其条件是：每人每月工资，飞行员600美元，队长750美元；机械人员250~400美元，每年30天带薪金休假，外加每月30美元生活津贴。每个志愿人员都必须签约作为中国空军志愿人员，为中国空军服务，并受到交战国被俘人员的国际保护。

AGREEMENT

THIS AGREEMENT made at ...San Diego...............this......6.......................day of ...August..............., 1941, by and between CENTRAL AIRCRAFT MANUFACTURING COMPANY, FEDERAL INC., U.S.A., 30 Rockefeller Plaza, New York, N. Y., a corporation organized under the Provisions of an Act of Congress known as "China Trade Act 1922", hereinafter called the Employer, and........ROBERT JAMES RAINES.. residing at...................Box 99, Route 1, Reno, Nevada.......................................hereinafter called the Employee

WITNESSETH that:

WHEREAS, the Employer among other things operates an aircraft manufacturing, operating and repair business in China, and

WHEREAS, the Employer desires to employ the Employee in connection with its business and said Employee desires to enter into such employment,

NOW THEREFORE, in consideration of the premises and the mutual covenants and agreements herein contained, it is agreed between the parties as follows:

ARTICLE 1. The Employer agrees to employ the Employee to render such services and perform such duties as the Employer may direct and the Employee agrees to enter the service of the Employer who, in consideration of the Employee's faithfully and diligently performing said duties and rendering said services, will pay to the Employee a salary of....six hundred dollars United States currency (U. S. $....600.00) per month payable monthly on the last business day of each calendar month.

ARTICLE 2. The said employment shall become effective and salary payments to the Employee therefor shall begin as from the date of the Employee's reporting in person to the Employer's representative at the port of departure from the United States (which port shall be designated to the Employee by the Employer), such date to be not later than ....August 28, 1941..........................., and shall continue for one year after the date on which the Employee shall arrive at the port of entry to China (which port shall be designated by the Employer to the Employee prior to the latter's departure from the United States) unless sooner terminated as hereinafter provided. The Employee undertakes to report to the Employer's representative at the said port of entry immediately upon arrival there. After the expiration of the said term of one year this contract shall continue in effect on the same terms and conditions unless and until terminated by either party on 30 days' written notice.

ARTICLE 3. The Employer agrees to pay all reasonable travel costs to the Employee from..........San Diego, Calif. to the place in China to which the Employee may be directed to proceed, including:

(a) First class railroad fare and berth, if necessary, by the most direct route to point of departure from the United States plus U. S. $3.00 per day for meals en route.

(b) Actual cost of passport and visas.

(c) Reasonable cost of hotel and meals while awaiting ocean transportation in accordance with travel instructions of the Employer.

(d) Transportation to port of entry to China.

(e) The sum of U. S. $100.00 for contingent expenses en route to port of entry.

(f) Actual expenses from the port of entry to the designated destination in China to be accounted for by the Employee to the Employer.

ARTICLE 4. At the expiration of this contract the Employer agrees to pay to the Employee in addition to the sums elsewhere stipulated in this contract the sum of U. S. $500.00 in lieu of Employee's return transportation costs from China to the United States.

ARTICLE 5. The Employer reserves the right to terminate this contract summarily by written notice to the Employee in the event of misconduct of the employee in any one of the following categories:

(a) Insubordination;

(b) Revealing confidential information;

(c) Habitual use of drugs;

(d) Excessive use of alcoholic liquors;

(e) Illness or other disability incurred not in line of duty and as a result of Employee's own misconduct; or

(f) Malingering.

In the event of termination of this contract for any of the causes above mentioned under (a) to (f) inclusive of this ARTICLE 5, the Employer shall not be obligated to pay the return travel allowance provided for in ARTICLE 4 above nor have any further obligations to the Employee under this contract except that the Employee shall be entitled to the earned portion of his salary computed to the date on which written notice of termination is given by the Employer under the provisions of this ARTICLE 5.

ARTICLE 6. In the event of the total disability or death of the Employee suffered in line of duty the Employer upon receipt of proof of such total disability or death shall immediately pay to the Employee or to the Employee's designated beneficiary as the case may be a sum equal to six months' salary at the monthly rate provided for in ARTICLE 1 hereof. In the event of total disability the Employer shall defray the expenses of transportation of the Employee to the United States. In the event of death the employer shall defray the expenses of a decent burial of the remains. The Employee agrees that he has in good standing a policy of U. S. Government Insurance in the amount of $10,000, Policy No.........................., plus disability benefits and hereby authorizes the Employer to pay the premiums on said insurance during the period of this employment and to deduct the amount of said premiums from the pay of said Employee.

ARTICLE 7. In addition to the payments provided for elsewhere in this contract, the Employer shall provide or cause to be provided to the Employee free of charge:

(a) Suitable living quarters or an allowance of U. S. $30.00 per month in lieu thereof.

(b) Necessary motor transportation.

(c) Suitable medical and dental service.

ARTICLE 8. The Employee shall be entitled to leave with pay as follows:

(a) One month's leave during the first year of employment at such time or times as his services can best be spared.

(b) Similarly in the event of additional service beyond the first year, leave for a period equal to 1/12 of the duration of such additional service.

(c) Sick leave with pay if and as necessary, not to exceed one month in any period of one year.

IN WITNESS WHEREOF the Employer and Employee have executed this agreement in quadruplicate, of which two copies are retained by each party.

CENTRAL AIRCRAFT MANUFACTURING COMPANY
FEDERAL INC., U. S. A.

.... By: ....
Witness

.... Robert J. Raines ....
Witness

【合同全文翻译】:

合 同

本合同于1941年8月6日签于圣地亚哥，签约双方为美国联邦中央飞机制造公司（地址为纽约洛克菲勒大厦30号，是按照国会“1922年对华贸易法案”的有关规定而组建的公司，以下称为雇主）与罗伯特·詹姆斯·雷恩（住址为内华达州里诺市1号大道99号信箱，以下称为雇员）。

谨共同见证:

鉴于雇主的业务之一是在中国制造、经营和修理飞机，

并鉴于雇主的愿望是在其业务中雇用雇员，而该雇员也愿意接受这样的雇用关系，

因此，考虑到其中所包含的前提条件以及相互间的合同与契约，双方谨达成以下协议:

条款1.雇主同意雇用雇员以从事雇主所指示的工作和职责，而雇员同意参加此工作，在雇员忠实勤恳地执行上述职责并完成上述服务后，雇主将支付雇员每月现金陆佰美元（U.S. $ 600.00）作为薪金，并于每个月的最后一个工作日发给。

条款2. 上述雇用关系将于雇员本人在美国出发港口向雇主代表报到时生效（出发港口将由雇主指定），薪金也同时由这天算起，此报到日期不得晚于1941年8月28日，并且此雇用关系从到达中国港口之日起延续一年（到达港口也将由雇主在雇员出发前指定），除非按下述条款雇用关系终止。雇员一经到达上述中国港口就应立即向雇主代表报到。在上述一年期满后该合同应在相同条款和条件下继续有效，除非其中任何一方在30天内以书面形式提出终止合同。

条款3.雇主同意支付雇员从加利福尼亚圣地亚哥市到中国工作地所需的所有差旅费，其中包括:

（a）头等火车票和卧铺，如有必要，以美国出发最短的路线计算，外加每天3美元的伙食费。

（b）护照和签证的实际费用。

（c）在与雇主的线路指示一致的情况下，由于等待海上运载所产生的合理的旅馆费用

和伙食费。

（d）进入中国港口的运载。

（e）在到达中国港口前途中的零用钱100美元。

（f）从中国港口前往中国指定地点的实际费用。

条款4.该合同期满后，除该合同规定的其他金额以外，雇主同意再付给雇员500美元，作为其从中国返回美国的交通费。

条款5.当雇员犯有以下任何一种不良行为时，雇主有权当即以书面形式终止合同：

（a）不服从；

（b）泄露保密信息；

（c）有吸毒的习惯；

（d）过度饮酒；

（e）由于雇员自己的不良行为而非执行公务时造成了疾病或伤残；

（f）装病；

由于条款5下（a）－（f）的原因而终止该合同的情况下，雇主没有义务付给雇员条款4所规定的津贴，也不再承担该合同中其他对雇员的义务，只结算根据条款5书面通知终止合同日之前的工资给雇员。

条款6. 当雇员在执行公务时完全失去工作能力或死亡的情况下，雇主一经确认就应立即支付给雇员或雇员所指定的受益人六个月的薪金，薪金数额已在条款1中加以规定。在完全失去工作能力的情况下，雇主应支付雇员返回美国的费用。在死亡的情况下，雇主应支付合理的丧葬费用。雇员同意自己持有有效的美国政府总额10,000美元的保险单，保险单编号__________，加上伤残福利，特此授权雇主代为缴纳上述雇用期间的保险费，并从雇员的薪金中扣除这部分费用。

条款7.除了本合同规定付给的报酬外，雇主还应免费向雇员提供：

（a）适当的住所或代之以每月30美元的津贴。

（b）必要的汽车运输。

（c）适当的医药和牙科服务。

条款8.雇员有权享受以下带薪休假：

（a）雇用的第一年在其任务许可的情况下一次性或分期休假一个月。

（b）一年以后延长期的服务，相应地可享受延长期月数1/12个月的休假。

（c）如有必要病休可带薪，但一年中不得超过一个月。

此合同共肆份，雇主和雇员各执贰份，以资证明。

美国联邦股份有限公司中央飞机制造公司

证人：（签字） 签约人：（公司代表签字）

证人：（签字） 罗伯特·J.雷恩（签字）

Background:At the end of 1940, Chennault and member of Aeronautical Commission Mao Bangchu sought out American fighters and recruited pilots. Their request was finally approved by President Franklin D. Roosevelt with the signing of the Lend-Lease Act on March 11th 1940. Combat aircraft and weaponry could be leased to China and other countries under the Act. On April 15th, 1941, a secret executive order went out under Roosevelt's approval, authorizing reserve officer and servicemen on active duty to resign from the Army Air Corps, Naval and Marine Air services for the purpose of joining the American Volunteer Group in China. The American Government lent 100 Curtiss P-40 fighters to China.

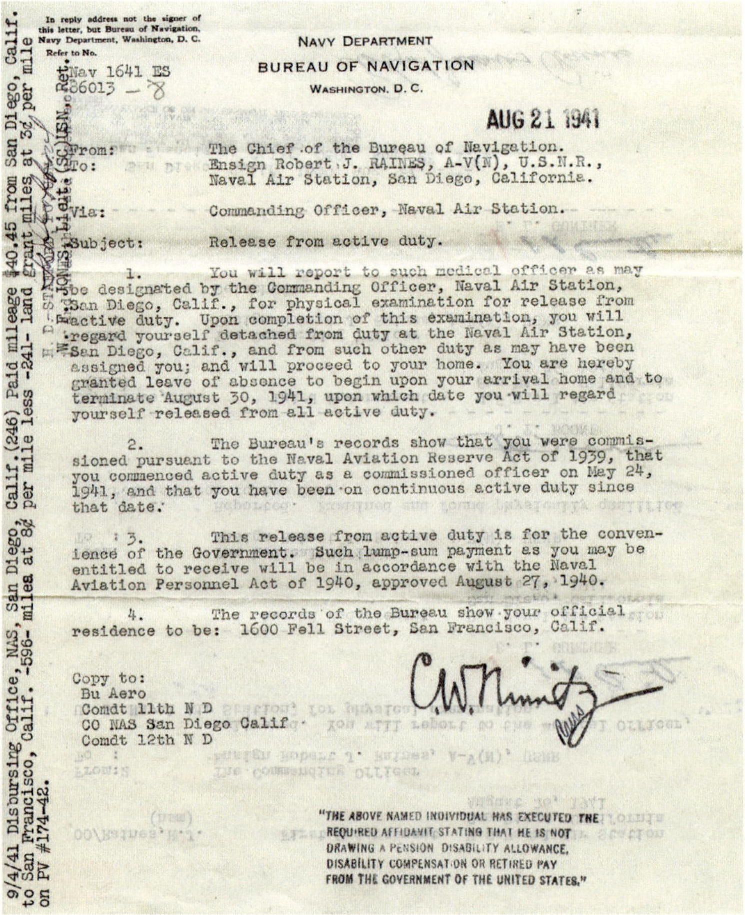

In reply address not the signer of this letter, but Bureau of Navigation, Navy Department, Washington, D. C.
Refer to No.
Nav 1641 ES
86013 – 8

NAVY DEPARTMENT
BUREAU OF NAVIGATION
WASHINGTON, D. C.

AUG 21 1941

From: The Chief of the Bureau of Navigation.
To: Ensign Robert J. RAINES, A-V(N), U.S.N.R., Naval Air Station, San Diego, California.

Via: Commanding Officer, Naval Air Station.

Subject: Release from active duty.

1. You will report to such medical officer as may be designated by the Commanding Officer, Naval Air Station, San Diego, Calif., for physical examination for release from active duty. Upon completion of this examination, you will regard yourself detached from duty at the Naval Air Station, San Diego, Calif., and from such other duty as may have been assigned you; and will proceed to your home. You are hereby granted leave of absence to begin upon your arrival home and to terminate August 30, 1941, upon which date you will regard yourself released from all active duty.

2. The Bureau's records show that you were commissioned pursuant to the Naval Aviation Reserve Act of 1939, that you commenced active duty as a commissioned officer on May 24, 1941, and that you have been on continuous active duty since that date.

3. This release from active duty is for the convenience of the Government. Such lump-sum payment as you may be entitled to receive will be in accordance with the Naval Aviation Personnel Act of 1940, approved August 27, 1940.

4. The records of the Bureau show your official residence to be: 1600 Fell Street, San Francisco, Calif.

C. W. Nimitz

Copy to:
Bu Aero
Comdt 11th N D
CO NAS San Diego Calif.
Comdt 12th N D

"THE ABOVE NAMED INDIVIDUAL HAS EXECUTED THE REQUIRED AFFIDAVIT STATING THAT HE IS NOT DRAWING A PENSION DISABILITY ALLOWANCE, DISABILITY COMPENSATION OR RETIRED PAY FROM THE GOVERNMENT OF THE UNITED STATES."

9/4/41 Disbursing Office, NAS, San Diego, Calif. (246) Paid mileage $40.45 from San Diego, Calif. to San Francisco, Calif. -596- miles at 8¢ per mile less -241- land grant miles at 3¢ per mile on PV #174-42.

该文件由美国海军部航海局长尼米兹签署，是雷恩从海军退役的文件。当时美国尚未向日本宣战，必须以平民身份来华，因此雷恩加入志愿队必须首先退出现役。美国军方对此给予了积极的支持，这份文件正是关于雷恩退出海军现役的有力物证。文件签署日期为1941年8月21日。当时雷恩位于加利福尼亚圣地亚哥海军航空站，少尉军衔。文件中明确了为加利福尼亚州圣地亚哥海军航空兵站现役退役人员体检、休假、补助金等事宜。在文件中记录雷恩的住址为加利福尼亚州旧金山菲尔街1600号。

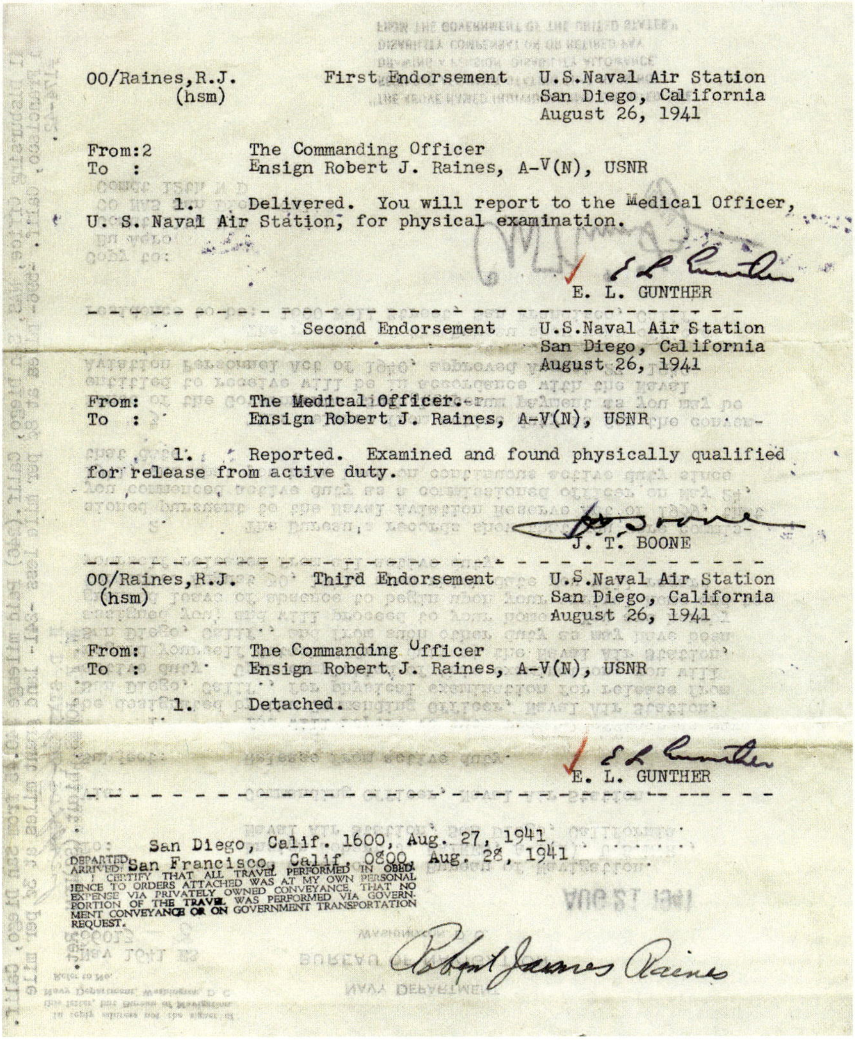

00/Raines,R.J. (hsm) First Endorsement U.S.Naval Air Station San Diego, California August 26, 1941

From:2 The Commanding Officer
To : Ensign Robert J. Raines, A-V(N), USNR

1. Delivered. You will report to the Medical Officer, U. S. Naval Air Station, for physical examination.

E. L. GUNTHER

Second Endorsement U.S.Naval Air Station San Diego, California August 26, 1941

From: The Medical Officer.
To : Ensign Robert J. Raines, A-V(N), USNR

1. Reported. Examined and found physically qualified for release from active duty.

J. T. BOONE

00/Raines,R.J. (hsm) Third Endorsement U.S.Naval Air Station San Diego, California August 26, 1941

From: The Commanding Officer
To : Ensign Robert J. Raines, A-V(N), USNR

1. Detached.

E. L. GUNTHER

DEPARTED San Diego, Calif. 1600, Aug. 27, 1941
ARRIVED San Francisco, Calif. 0800, Aug. 28, 1941
I CERTIFY THAT ALL TRAVEL PERFORMED IN OBEDIENCE TO ORDERS ATTACHED WAS AT MY OWN PERSONAL EXPENSE VIA PRIVATELY OWNED CONVEYANCE, THAT NO PORTION OF THE TRAVEL WAS PERFORMED VIA GOVERNMENT CONVEYANCE OR ON GOVERNMENT TRANSPORTATION REQUEST.

Robert James Raines

This document was issued on August 21st, 1941, signed by Chester William Nimitz, the Chief of Bureau of Navigation. The document confirmed Raine's release from active duty at The Naval Air Station.

Since the United States was not yet at war with Japan, Raine had to assume civilian status in order to join the AVG and travel to China.

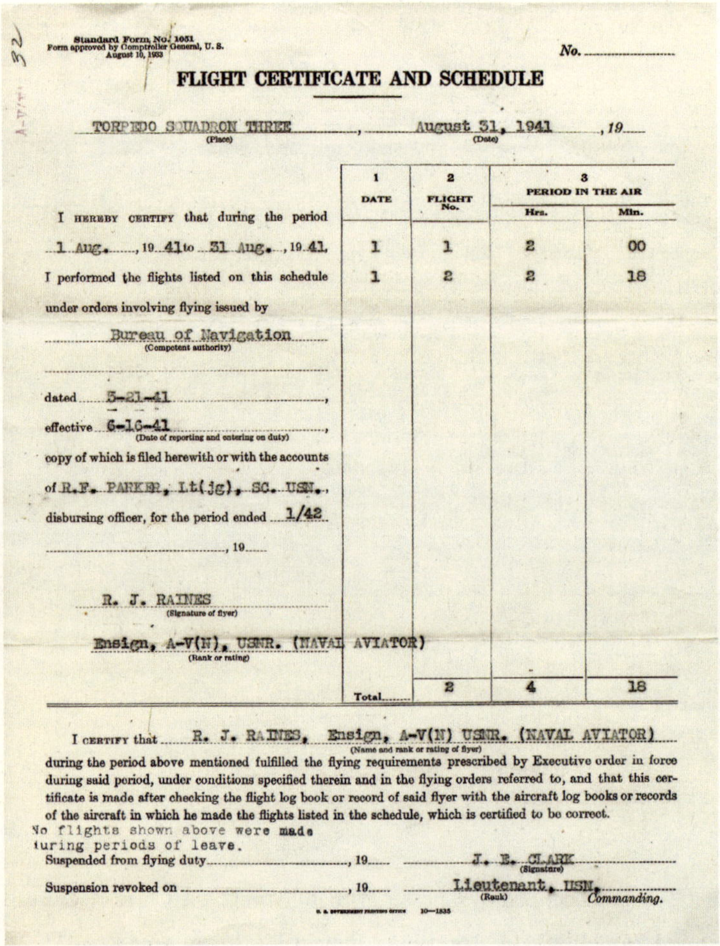

Standard Form No. 1051
Form approved by Comptroller General, U. S.
August 10, 1933

No. ....

FLIGHT CERTIFICATE AND SCHEDULE

TORPEDO SQUADRON THREE (Place), August 31, 1941 (Date), 19

I HEREBY CERTIFY that during the period 1 Aug., 19 41 to 31 Aug., 19 41, I performed the flights listed on this schedule under orders involving flying issued by Bureau of Navigation (Competent authority) dated 5-21-41, effective 6-16-41 (Date of reporting and entering on duty), copy of which is filed herewith or with the accounts of R.F. PARKER, Lt(jg), SC. USN., disbursing officer, for the period ended 1/42 ...., 19....

R. J. RAINES (Signature of flyer)

Ensign, A-V(N), USNR. (NAVAL AVIATOR) (Rank or rating)

1 DATE	2 FLIGHT No.	3 PERIOD IN THE AIR Hrs.	Min.
1	1	2	00
1	2	2	18
Total......	2	4	18

I CERTIFY that R. J. RAINES, Ensign, A-V(N) USNR. (NAVAL AVIATOR) (Name and rank or rating of flyer) during the period above mentioned fulfilled the flying requirements prescribed by Executive order in force during said period, under conditions specified therein and in the flying orders referred to, and that this certificate is made after checking the flight log book or record of said flyer with the aircraft log books or records of the aircraft in which he made the flights listed in the schedule, which is certified to be correct.

No flights shown above were made during periods of leave.

Suspended from flying duty ...., 19.... J. B. CLARK (Signature)

Suspension revoked on ...., 19.... Lieutenant, USN, (Rank) *Commanding.*

U. S. GOVERNMENT PRINTING OFFICE 10—1835

雷恩的飞行记录显示：雷恩所在的编队为鱼雷三中队。此飞行记录的日期是1941年8月31日，反映雷恩在航空局颁发的导航命令下，执行日程表上所列航班的任务。1941年8月1日至8月31日期间，雷恩共计飞行4小时18分钟。该飞行记录证明雷恩在规定的条件下和航空局指令有效期内完成了规定内需要完成的飞行任务，是考评飞行员的飞行记录簿。

Raine's Flight Record

雷恩的人寿保险合同

Raine's Life Insurance Policy

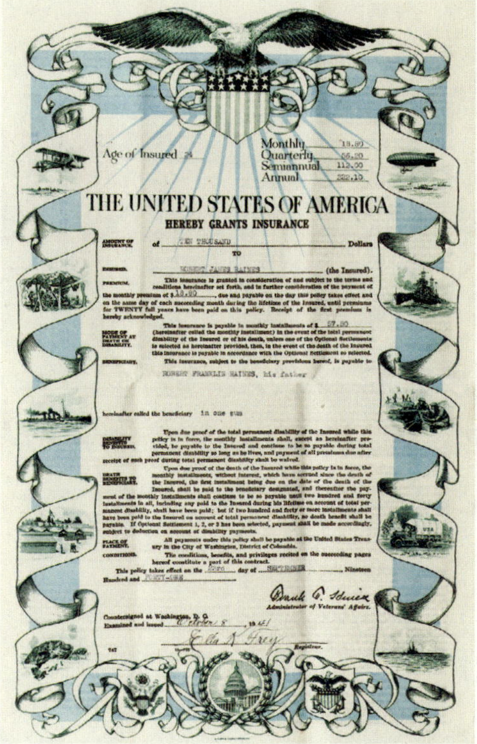

Age of Insured 24

Monthly 18.80
Quarterly 56.20
Semiannual 112.00
Annual 222.15

THE UNITED STATES OF AMERICA
HEREBY GRANTS INSURANCE

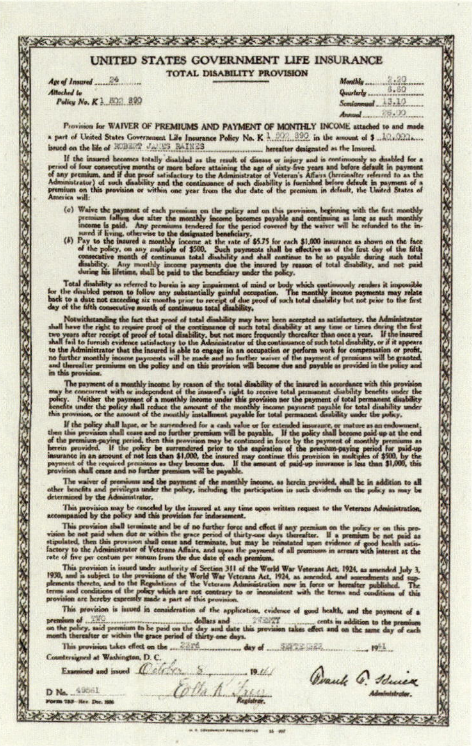

UNITED STATES GOVERNMENT LIFE INSURANCE
TOTAL DISABILITY PROVISION

雷恩的人寿保险合同，被保险人为雷恩，当时雷恩24岁，投保日期为1941年10月8日，保险为人寿险附加伤残险，保险金额为10000美金。投保人和受益人均为雷恩的父亲，保险合同上有其父罗伯特·弗兰克林·雷恩的签名。人寿保险的购买在雷恩与美国联邦中央飞机制造公司签订合约中有所提及，保险费由雇主即美国联邦中央飞机制造公司缴纳，之后从雷恩的薪金中扣除。

Raine's life insurance policy was issued on October 8th, 1941, while he was 24. Both policyholder and beneficiary was Raine's father, Robert Franklin Raine. The policy was life insurance plus additional invalidity insurance. This policy was mentioned in the contract of employment signed by Raine and the Central Aircraft Manufacturing Company (CAMCO).

从旧金山寄出给雷恩的信封

The envelope sent from San Francisco to Raine

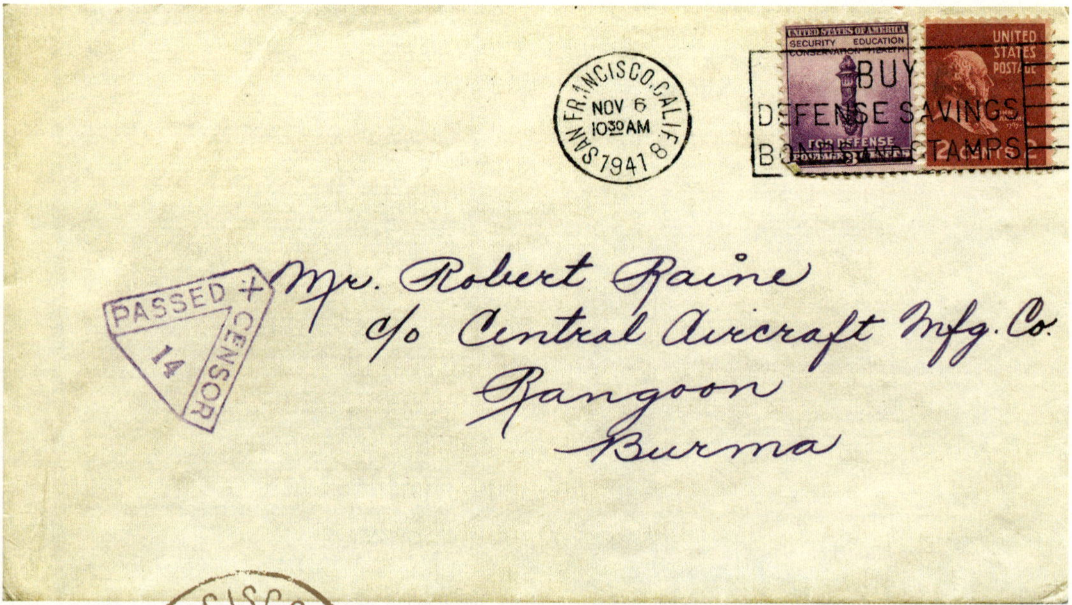

信封上的邮戳表明信件是1941年11月6日寄出，寄给当时在缅甸仰光的雷恩，由美国联邦中央飞机制造公司转交。虽然当时美国志愿队已经成立，但队员对外公开身份仍是美国联邦中央飞机制造公司的雇员。

The stamp on the envelope indicated the letter was mailed-out on November 6th, 1941, and sent to Raine while he was in Rangoon, Burma; forwarded by the U.S. Federal Central Aircraft Manufacturing Company. Although the American Volunteer Group had been established, the volunteers' public identity were still the employees of the U.S. Federal Central Aircraft Manufacturing Company.

缅甸政府发给雷恩的免签证明

Certificate of Exemption

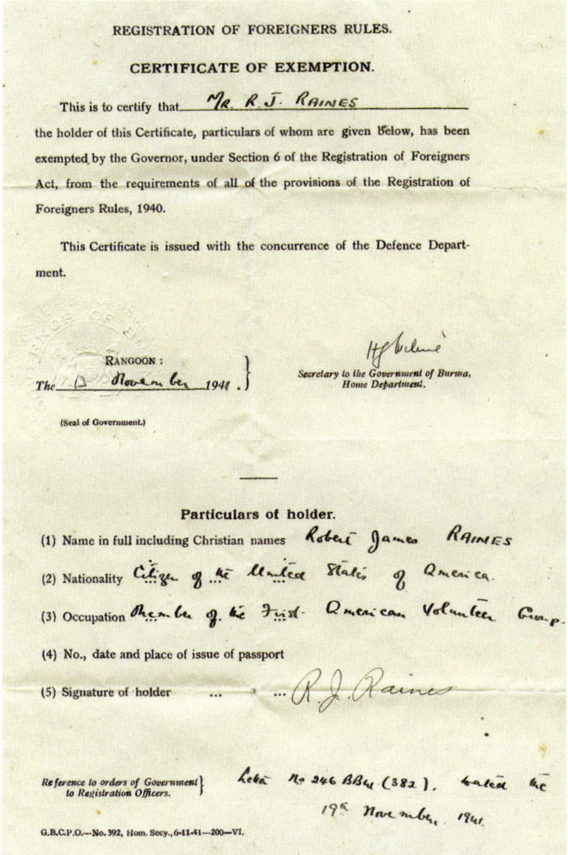

REGISTRATION OF FOREIGNERS RULES.

CERTIFICATE OF EXEMPTION.

This is to certify that Mr. R. J. RAINES the holder of this Certificate, particulars of whom are given below, has been exempted by the Governor, under Section 6 of the Registration of Foreigners Act, from the requirements of all of the provisions of the Registration of Foreigners Rules, 1940.

This Certificate is issued with the concurrence of the Defence Department.

RANGOON: The 13 November 1941.

Secretary to the Government of Burma, Home Department.

(Seal of Government.)

Particulars of holder.

(1) Name in full including Christian names Robert James RAINES

(2) Nationality Citizen of the United States of America

(3) Occupation Member of the First American Volunteer Group

(4) No., date and place of issue of passport

(5) Signature of holder ... ... R. J. Raines

Reference to orders of Government to Registration Officers. Letter No 246 BBM (382), dated the 19th November 1941.

G.B.C.P.O.—No. 392, Hom. Secy., 6-11-41—200—VI.

该证明由缅甸政府内务部签发，国防部认定，准许雷恩免签入境。证书上详细记录有雷恩的姓名、国籍，职业一栏则写明为美国志愿队（AVG），下有雷恩亲笔签名。1941年11月，是雷恩到达缅甸仰光的时间。志愿队员集结缅甸仰光后，队员的身份可以明示。

The Certificate of Exemption was issued by the Burma Government with concurrence of the defense department to Raine. It allowed Raine enter Burma without a visa.

苏公望给雷恩的请柬
Invitation for Mr. Raine from General So Kung-Mon.

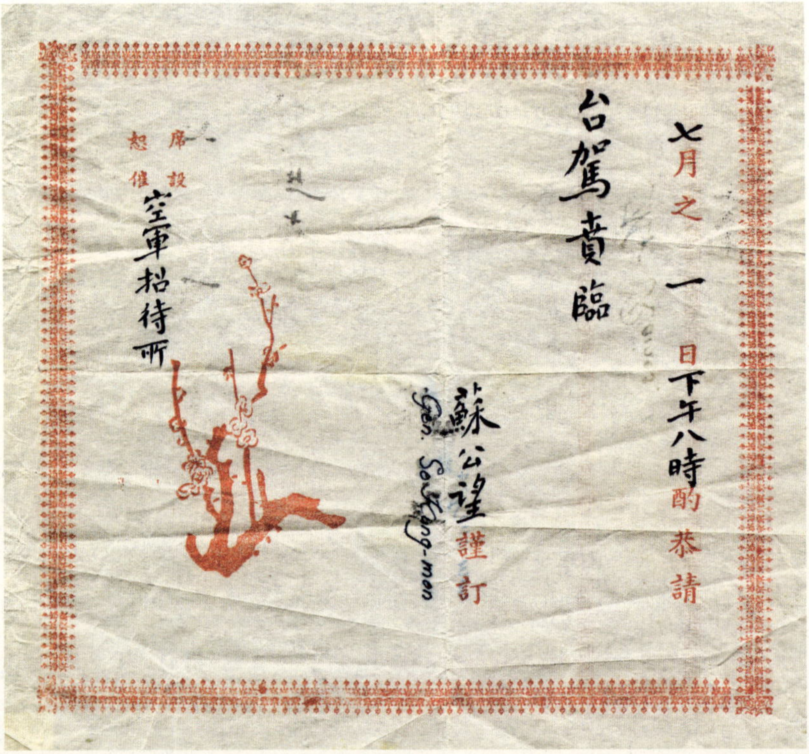
七月之一日下午八時酌恭請
台駕賁臨
蘇公望謹訂
Gen. So Kung-mon
席設空軍招待所
恕催

纸质请柬，正文外镶嵌红色花边，内装饰有梅花图案。正文内容如下：“七月一日下午八时酌恭请台驾贲临　苏公望谨订　席设空军招待所　恕催”。正文背面花纹框内，有钢笔书写英文“Mr Raines”字样。

【背景知识】：苏公望，原名苏辕，曾用名龚放，1902年7月出生于湖南湘潭。1924年11月，考入广东建国湘军讲武堂第一期学习，并加入国民党。1933年3月起，苏公望先后任上海市防空协会总干事、防空总监部防空情报处副处长、防空学校防空情报班主任等职。其间，参与了国民政府的防空创建规划和指挥对日防空作战。1942年5月，协同美军“飞虎队”在衡阳展开对日空战。1949年8月苏公望参加湖南和平起义，后任中国人民解放军长沙警备司令部高参、湖南省军区司令部高参。1952年3月任湖南省人民政府参事室参事。

Background: So Kung-Mon, original name Su Yuan, previous name Gong Fang, was born in Xiangtan, Hunan Province in July, 1902. He was admitted to Jianguo Xiangjun Military Academy in Guangdong Province as one of the first batch of cadets in November, 1924 and joined Kuomintang there. In March 1933, So Kung-Mon was appointed the general secretary of Air Defense Association of Shanghai; deputy director of Air Defense Intelligence under General Administration of Air Defense, director of Air Defense Intelligence class of the Air Defense Academy. During that period, he took part in the creation of Kuomintang government's air defense network and took command of the air defense against Japanese air force. In May 1942, So collaborated with the Flying Tigers in the air battle of Hengyang, Hunan Province. In August 1949, So took part in the peaceful surrender in Hunan province to the Communists army. After the establishment of the People's Republic of China, he was appointed to high-ranking positions, such as in the member of the Chief of Staff Department of Changsha Garrison Headquarters, and as a member of the Chief of Staff Department of Hunan Provincial Military Zone. In March 1952, So became an advisor in the Advisory Department of Hunan Provincial Government.

DIARY

BOMBING REPORT

DATE : 5/27/42.
PLACE: Kunming.

PILOT:	R. J. Raines.	AIRPLANE:	P-40E.
SQUADRON:	2nd Pursuit Squadron.	MAPS USED:	Tali Section.
DESIGNATION:	Wing Man.	TYPE MISSION:	Bombing mission.

TIME OF DEPARTURE: 1330   TIME OF RETURN: 1700.

OBJECTIVE-ROUTE OR AREA COVERED: Kunming, YunnanYi, Paoshan, Mengshih, Lunling, YunnanYi and Kunming. Objective was Mengshih and Lunling.
ENEMY AIRCRAFT ENCOUNTERED: None.

GROUND ACTION OF ENEMY WHEN ATTACK: None.

ENEMY LOSSES: None.

DAMAGE TO PILOTS AIRCRAFT: None.

ALLIED LOSSES OBSERVED: None.

PILOTS AMMUNITION EXPENDED: Ammo: None. Bombs: six thirty-five pound bombs.

DURATION OF FLIGHT: 3 hours and 30 minutes.

REMARKS:-----

We left Kunming at approximately 1330. Refueled at YunnanYi and after three Chinese Bombers had passed overhead we took off and rendezvoued over Paoshan. The Chinese Bombers were at 10,000 feet, Rector, Bright, Conant and myself were at 11,000 feet while Neale of the First Pursuit Squadron with three others remained at 16,000 feet as top cover, preceeded to Mengshih where the Chinese Bombers dropped their bombs hitting in the center of town. Rector and his flight then went to Lunling where the four of us dropped our bombs. All bursts were in the town of Lunling, one string hitting on the main street.

Conant became seperated from the flight over Lunling , I could see him so he and I came to YunnanYi and landed. We were soon joined there by Rector and Bright. I was supposed to rendezvous over Paoshan but because of bad radio reception went straight to YunnanYi. The four of us together returned to Kunming from YunnanYi.

If the purpose of the mission called for hits on Lunling then it was highly successfull.

SIGNED: R. J. Raines.

时间：1942年5月27日	地点：昆明
飞行员：R.J.雷恩	机型：P-40E
中队：第2驱逐中队	使用地图：大理部分
行动代号：翼人	任务类型：执行轰炸
离港时间：13：30	返港时间：17：00
目标——航线及覆盖区域：昆明 云南驿 保山 芒市 龙陵 云南驿 昆明	
轰炸目标：芒市 龙陵	遭遇敌机：否
是否遭遇敌人地面攻击：否	敌军损失：无
驾驶飞机损失情况：无	盟军损失观察：无
飞行员弹药使用情况：投弹——6枚，35磅	交换机——无
战斗持续时间：3小时30分	

摘要：

我们大约于13：30分离开昆明，在云南驿加油，等中国的三架轰炸机从上空飞过后，我们起飞并在保山上空的指定地点汇合。中方轰炸机在10000英尺高度，Rector、Bright柯南特和我在11000英尺高度，而此时，第一驱逐中队的尼尔正和其他三位飞行员保持在16000英尺的高度担任高空掩护。我们继续飞往芒市，在那里中国轰炸机丢下的炸弹击中市镇中心区域。接着，Rector和他的飞机飞往龙陵，并在那里投下4枚炸弹，所有爆炸都在龙陵境内，成串的打击落在中心街区。

柯南特从龙陵的飞行中分离出来，我能够看到他。之后，他和我飞往云南驿并在此降落。不久之后，Rector和Bright加入了我们。我预定的汇合地点在保山，但依据雷达接收到的信号我直飞云南驿。我们四人一起从云南驿返航昆明。如果这次任务的目标是完成打击，那么它是非常成功的。

签名：R.J.雷恩

雷恩的收入清单说明

The Notice of Salary Payment to all Group Personnel from AVG Finance office

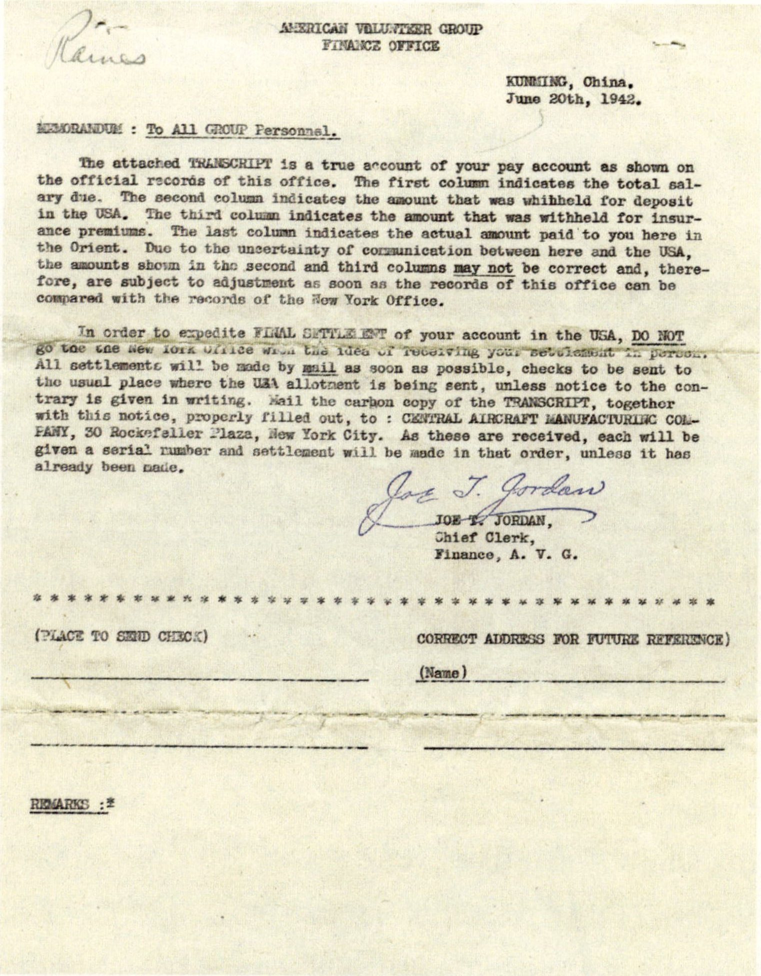

Raines

AMERICAN VOLUNTEER GROUP
FINANCE OFFICE

KUNMING, China.
June 20th, 1942.

MEMORANDUM : To All GROUP Personnel.

The attached TRANSCRIPT is a true account of your pay account as shown on the official records of this office. The first column indicates the total salary due. The second column indicates the amount that was withheld for deposit in the USA. The third column indicates the amount that was withheld for insurance premiums. The last column indicates the actual amount paid to you here in the Orient. Due to the uncertainty of communication between here and the USA, the amounts shown in the second and third columns may not be correct and, therefore, are subject to adjustment as soon as the records of this office can be compared with the records of the New York Office.

In order to expedite FINAL SETTLEMENT of your account in the USA, DO NOT go to the New York Office with the idea of receiving your settlement in person. All settlements will be made by mail as soon as possible, checks to be sent to the usual place where the USA allotment is being sent, unless notice to the contrary is given in writing. Mail the carbon copy of the TRANSCRIPT, together with this notice, properly filled out, to : CENTRAL AIRCRAFT MANUFACTURING COMPANY, 30 Rockefeller Plaza, New York City. As these are received, each will be given a serial number and settlement will be made in that order, unless it has already been made.

Joe T. Jordan
JOE T. JORDAN,
Chief Clerk,
Finance, A. V. G.

* *

(PLACE TO SEND CHECK) CORRECT ADDRESS FOR FUTURE REFERENCE)

(Name)

REMARKS :

美国志愿队财政部1942年6月20日给每个志愿队员的收入清单说明，由志愿队财务总管乔丹签发。此说明对收入清单的栏目逐一进行说明，如有与实际发放不一致的，财务部将与纽约办公室核对后调整。此说明还要求志愿队员将收入清单和说明一并寄回位于纽约市洛克菲勒广场30号的美国联邦中央飞机制造公司总部进行核对。

The Notice issued by Chief Clerk of Finance AVG, attached with a transcript of salary payment.

雷恩在志愿队期间的收入清单

The Transcript of salary payment made to personnel in the Orient

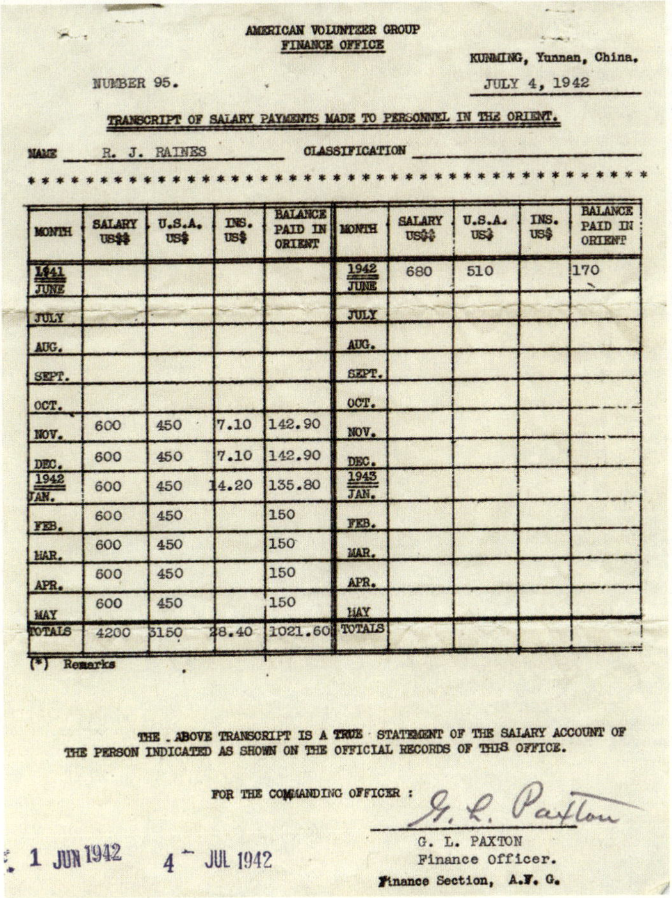

AMERICAN VOLUNTEER GROUP
FINANCE OFFICE

KUNMING, Yunnan, China.

NUMBER 95.

JULY 4, 1942

TRANSCRIPT OF SALARY PAYMENTS MADE TO PERSONNEL IN THE ORIENT.

NAME R. J. RAINES CLASSIFICATION

* *

MONTH	SALARY US$	U.S.A. US$	INS. US$	BALANCE PAID IN ORIENT	MONTH	SALARY US$	U.S.A. US$	INS. US$	BALANCE PAID IN ORIENT
1941 JUNE					1942 JUNE	680	510		170
JULY					JULY				
AUG.					AUG.				
SEPT.					SEPT.				
OCT.					OCT.				
NOV.	600	450	7.10	142.90	NOV.				
DEC.	600	450	7.10	142.90	DEC.				
1942 JAN.	600	450	14.20	135.80	1943 JAN.				
FEB.	600	450		150	FEB.				
MAR.	600	450		150	MAR.				
APR.	600	450		150	APR.				
MAY	600	450		150	MAY				
TOTALS	4200	3150	28.40	1021.60	TOTALS				

(*) Remarks

THE ABOVE TRANSCRIPT IS A TRUE STATEMENT OF THE SALARY ACCOUNT OF THE PERSON INDICATED AS SHOWN ON THE OFFICIAL RECORDS OF THIS OFFICE.

FOR THE COMMANDING OFFICER : G. L. Paxton

G. L. PAXTON
Finance Officer.
Finance Section, A.V.G.

1 JUN 1942 4 JUL 1942

The transcript made to Raine by Finance Section of The American Volunteer Group, issued in Kunming, Yunnan China on July 4th 1942.

此收入清单是经过核实无误，由美国志愿队财务主管帕克斯顿签发正式单据。清单上表明雷恩为第95号，收入发放截止到1942年7月4日，该时间是美国志愿队解散的时间。根据清单所列收入发放记录，证明雷恩从1941年11月至1942年7月4日隶属美国志愿队。收入为每月600美元，与同美国联邦中央飞机制造公司签订合约中约定的收入金额一致。600美元的收入中，450元寄往美国，代扣1941年11月至1942年1月三个月的保险费，其余为雷恩在中国的实际收入。1942年7月收入不满一月，按日计酬，每日为20美元，所以1942年6月的收入为680元。

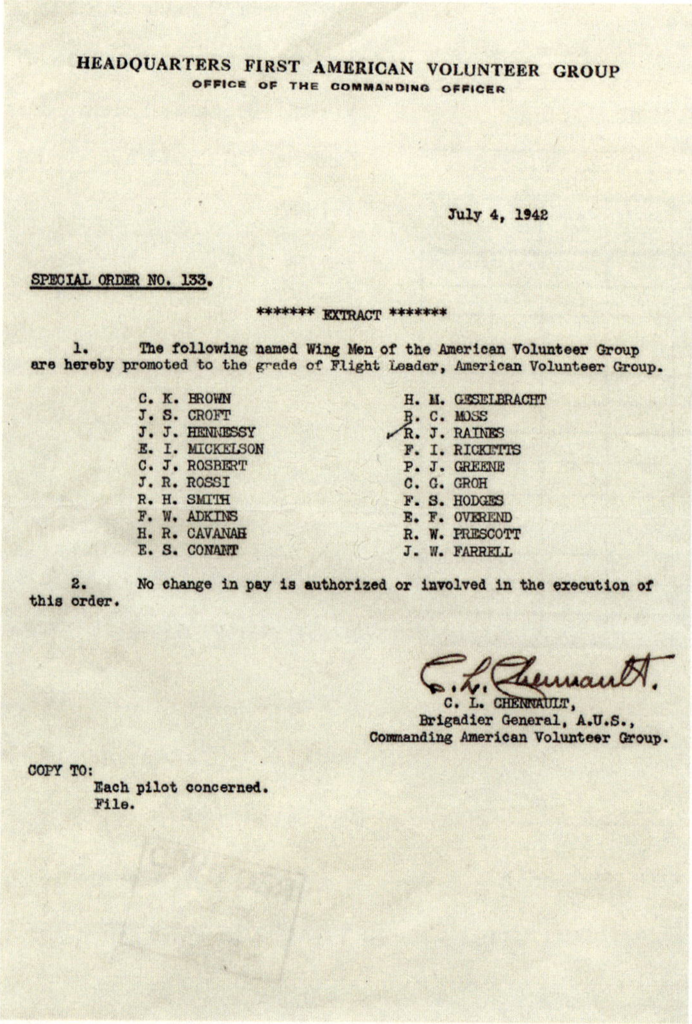

HEADQUARTERS FIRST AMERICAN VOLUNTEER GROUP
OFFICE OF THE COMMANDING OFFICER

July 4, 1942

SPECIAL ORDER NO. 133.

******* EXTRACT *******

1. The following named Wing Men of the American Volunteer Group are hereby promoted to the grade of Flight Leader, American Volunteer Group.

C. K. BROWN	H. M. GESELBRACHT
J. S. CROFT	R. C. MOSS
J. J. HENNESSY	R. J. RAINES
E. I. MICKELSON	F. I. RICKETTS
C. J. ROSBERT	P. J. GREENE
J. R. ROSSI	C. G. GROH
R. H. SMITH	F. S. HODGES
F. W. ADKINS	E. F. OVEREND
H. R. CAVANAH	R. W. PRESCOTT
E. S. CONANT	J. W. FARRELL

2. No change in pay is authorized or involved in the execution of this order.

C. L. Chennault.
C. L. CHENNAULT,
Brigadier General, A.U.S.,
Commanding American Volunteer Group.

COPY TO:
Each pilot concerned.
File.

由陈纳德亲笔签署的20名志愿队员荣升为飞机领航员的文件，雷恩也位列其中，其名字在右列三排。文件是1942年7月4日志愿队解散之日签发的，文件规定荣升为飞机领航员的队员收入不变。

The Order issued by C. L. Chennault. Raine was one of 20 Wing Man of A.V.G. promoted to the grade of Flight Leader of AVG.

中国空军美国志愿队队员衬衫
The uniform (shirt) of The American Volunteer Group

The uniform (shirt) of The American Volunteer Group

这是雷恩参加中国空军美国志愿队的物证。棉质，军绿色，长袖开衫衬衫，胸部左右有口袋各一，衣两侧圆摆开叉。衣领左领尖绣黄色飞行翼章，右领尖绣有英文美国志愿队缩写标志“AVG”。此类衣物存世量较少，弥足珍贵。

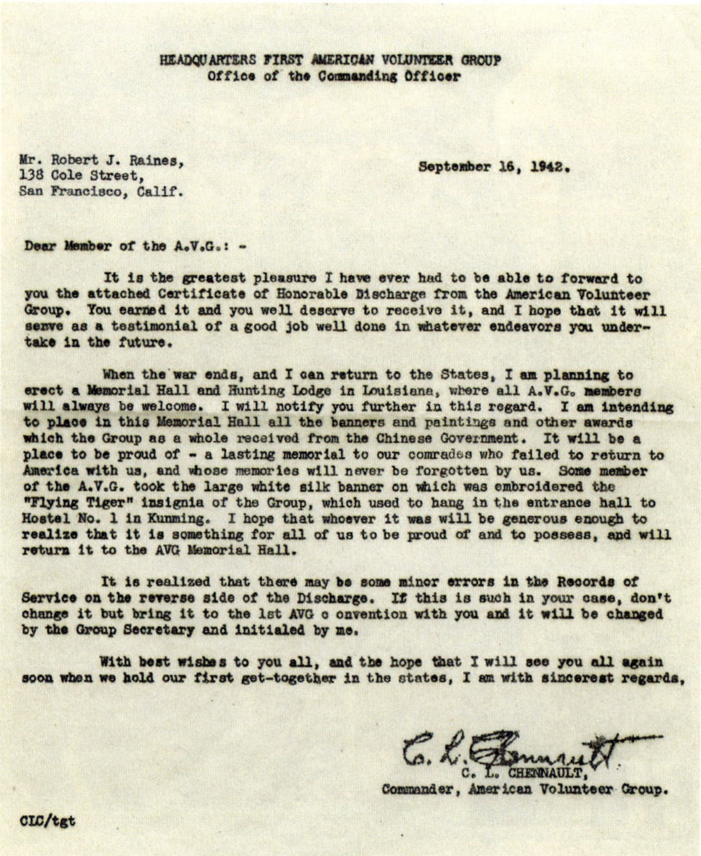

HEADQUARTERS FIRST AMERICAN VOLUNTEER GROUP
Office of the Commanding Officer

Mr. Robert J. Raines,
138 Cole Street,
San Francisco, Calif.

September 16, 1942.

Dear Member of the A.V.G.: -

It is the greatest pleasure I have ever had to be able to forward to you the attached Certificate of Honorable Discharge from the American Volunteer Group. You earned it and you well deserve to receive it, and I hope that it will serve as a testimonial of a good job well done in whatever endeavors you undertake in the future.

When the war ends, and I can return to the States, I am planning to erect a Memorial Hall and Hunting Lodge in Louisiana, where all A.V.G. members will always be welcome. I will notify you further in this regard. I am intending to place in this Memorial Hall all the banners and paintings and other awards which the Group as a whole received from the Chinese Government. It will be a place to be proud of - a lasting memorial to our comrades who failed to return to America with us, and whose memories will never be forgotten by us. Some member of the A.V.G. took the large white silk banner on which was embroidered the "Flying Tiger" insignia of the Group, which used to hang in the entrance hall to Hostel No. 1 in Kunming. I hope that whoever it was will be generous enough to realize that it is something for all of us to be proud of and to possess, and will return it to the AVG Memorial Hall.

It is realized that there may be some minor errors in the Records of Service on the reverse side of the Discharge. If this is such in your case, don't change it but bring it to the 1st AVG c onvention with you and it will be changed by the Group Secretary and initialed by me.

With best wishes to you all, and the hope that I will see you all again soon when we hold our first get-together in the states, I am with sincerest regards,

C. L. Chennault
C. L. CHENNAULT,
Commander, American Volunteer Group.

CLC/tgt

The letter signed by Commander C. L. Chennault, attached the Certificate of Honorable Discharge from A.V.G.

信是志愿队总部指挥官陈纳德办公室发出，给每一个志愿队成员的。每封信都有陈纳德的亲笔签名。日期为1942年9月16日，即志愿队解散3个月之后。信件左上雷恩的地址为加利福尼亚旧金山科尔街138号。信中告知队员随信附有志愿队颁发给每一位志愿队员的荣誉证书。信上说等战争结束，陈纳德指挥官将回到美国，在路易斯安那州建立志愿队的纪念堂，希望队员们把中国政府颁发的各种荣誉勋章及证书以及队旗等放到那里，让纪念堂也成为一个纪念牺牲队员的场所。信中还提到希望将原来悬挂于昆明第一招待所门口的飞虎标志也放入纪念堂。最后对志愿队在记录和服务工作中的一些小失误表示遗憾，有错误的情况希望队员联系志愿队秘书处。

雷恩照片底片

Raine's films

照片

底片

照片底片一卷，为负片胶卷，是雷恩保留的纪念胶卷，胶卷内保存7张照片，均为战友照片。

7 negative film images of his comrades-in-arms.

雷恩保留的求救血符

A blood chit

求救血符，白布地，上部为美国国旗图案，中下部为中、缅、印等多国文字，文字的内容均为寻求救援的内容。中文内容如下：“我是同盟国的战斗员，马来亚的民众是我的朋友，我绝不会来伤害你们的；我的目的是要打倒日本军，把他们赶出马来亚去。假定你们可以帮助我，等日本兵打退以后政府一定会重赏你们的。”

【背景知识】：求救血符在战争中发挥了重要作用。求救血符又称“血幅”、“救命符”。求救血符一般都缝制在部队配发的夹克里，一般约有一张手帕大小，有两种不同的形式。一种形式是上半部分是国民党当局的青天白日旗，下面写着“来华助战洋人，军民一体救护”等字样，当时的“飞虎队”的美国队员都配发了这种求生布条，一旦被迫跳伞落到地面，飞行员便可用它来与当地百姓沟通，请求救助。求救血符还有一种形式是美军制作的印有美国国旗的求救血符，并有中缅印等多国文字，文字大意是“我们是美国空军，来华助战打日本鬼子，请把我们送到有中国国民党军队或者有美国人的地方”，这种血符大多用于二战中缅印战区。这小小的求救血符，在二战中挽救了许多美国飞行员的宝贵生命，谱写了中美军民联合抗战、血肉相连的历史篇章，如今已经成为中美两国并肩战斗的历史见证。

Background: The blood chits played an important role in the war. The handkerchief-sized chits were usually patched onto the flight jackets of the aircrew. There were two types of chits. One had the flag of KMT government, and below it the Chinese characters saying “this foreign person has come to China to help in the war effort. Soldiers and civilians, one and all, should rescue, protect, and provide him medical care.” Every Flying Tigers pilot was issued a blood chit used to communicate with local people and seek for help in case he was forced to parachute. Another type of chit had the USA flag with Chinese, Burmese, and Indian languages. The texts basically said that “We are American pilot, fighting side by side with Chinese against Japanese. Please guide us to where Chinese army or Americans are stationed.” Most of these chits were used in the China Burma India Theatre. The blood chits helped save a lot of American pilots’ lives and reflected the valiancy and alliance of American and Chinese army during WWII.

雷恩印度的临时身份通行证

Temporary identity pass

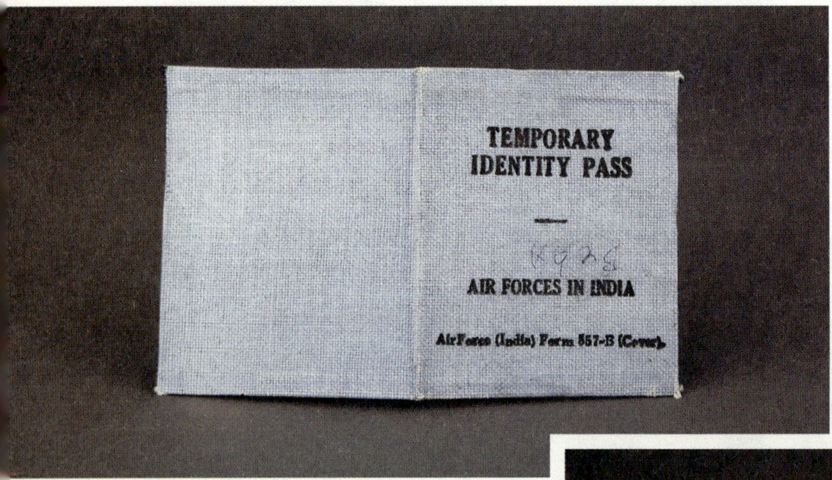

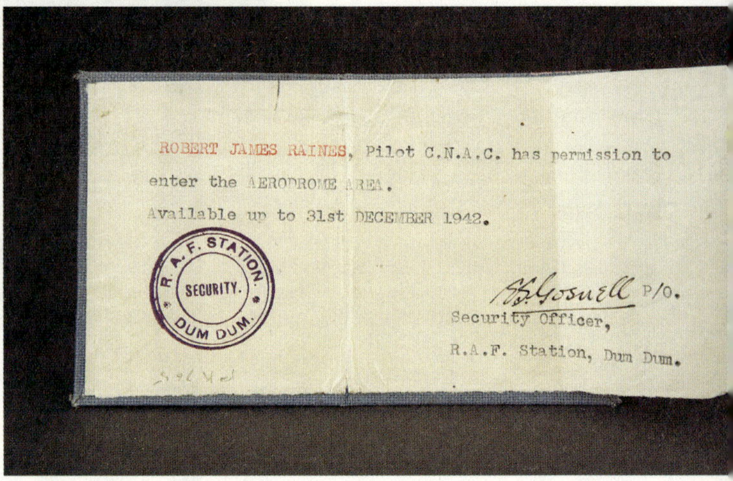

这是印度达姆达姆英国皇家空军基地发给已经成为中国航空公司飞行员的雷恩进入机场区域的临时身份通行证，有效期到1942年12月31日。

A temporary identity pass to the aerodrome area of R.A.F Station at Dum Dum, India issued to Robert Raine.

第2航空中队给雷恩等三人的行动命令

Operation order and invoice

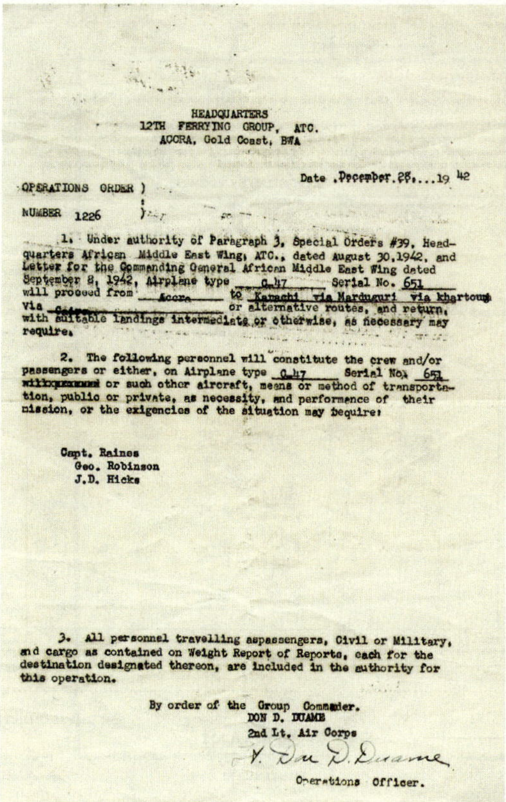

HEADQUARTERS
12TH FERRYING GROUP, ATC.
ACCRA, Gold Coast, BWA

Date .December.28....19 42

OPERATIONS ORDER)
:
NUMBER 1226)

1. Under authority of Paragraph 3, Special Orders #39, Headquarters African Middle East Wing, ATC., dated August 30,1942, and Letter for the Commanding General African Middle East Wing dated September 8, 1942, Airplane type C-47 Serial No. 651 will proceed from Accra to Karachi via Marduguri via khartoum via ~~Cairo~~ or alternative routes, and return, with suitable landings intermediate or otherwise, as necessary may require.

2. The following personnel will constitute the crew and/or passengers or either, on Airplane type C-47 Serial No. 651 [redacted] or such other aircraft, means or method of transportation, public or private, as necessity, and performance of their mission, or the exigencies of the situation may require:

Capt. Raines
Geo. Robinson
J.D. Hicks

3. All personnel travelling aspassengers, Civil or Military, and cargo as contained on Weight Report of Reports, each for the destination designated thereon, are included in the authority for this operation.

By order of the Group Commander.
DON D. DUAME
2nd Lt. Air Corps
Don D. Duame
Operations Officer.

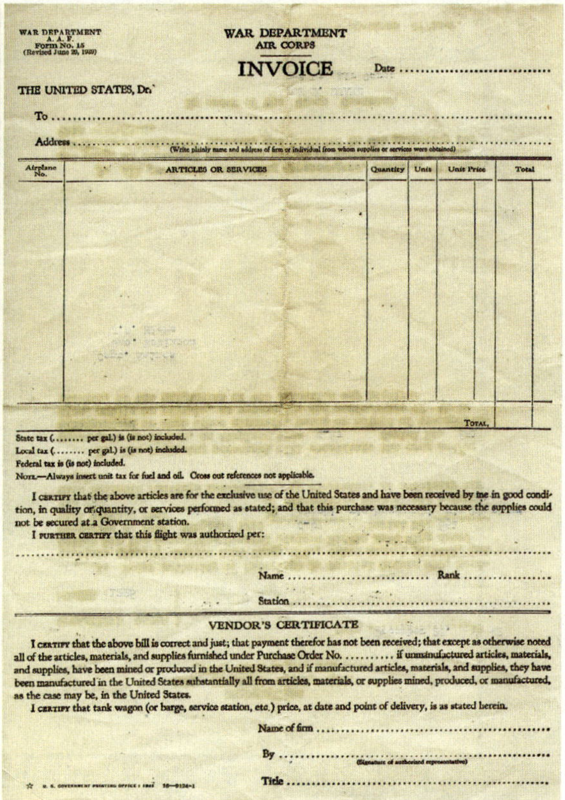

WAR DEPARTMENT
A. A. F.
Form No. 15
(Revised June 20, 1939)

WAR DEPARTMENT
AIR CORPS

INVOICE

Date ....

THE UNITED STATES, Dr.

To ....

Address ....
(Write plainly name and address of firm or individual from whom supplies or services were obtained)

Airplane No.	ARTICLES OR SERVICES	Quantity	Units	Unit Price	Total
				TOTAL,	

State tax (........ per gal.) is (is not) included.
Local tax (........ per gal.) is (is not) included.
Federal tax is (is not) included.
NOTE.—Always insert unit tax for fuel and oil. Cross out references not applicable.

I CERTIFY that the above articles are for the exclusive use of the United States and have been received by me in good condition, in quality or quantity, or services performed as stated; and that this purchase was necessary because the supplies could not be secured at a Government station.

I FURTHER CERTIFY that this flight was authorized per:

....

Name .... Rank ....

Station ....

VENDOR'S CERTIFICATE

I CERTIFY that the above bill is correct and just; that payment therefor has not been received; that except as otherwise noted all of the articles, materials, and supplies furnished under Purchase Order No. .... if unmanufactured articles, materials, and supplies, have been mined or produced in the United States, and if manufactured articles, materials, and supplies, they have been manufactured in the United States substantially all from articles, materials, or supplies mined, produced, or manufactured, as the case may be, in the United States.

I CERTIFY that tank wagon (or barge, service station, etc.) price, at date and point of delivery, is as stated herein.

Name of firm ....

By ....
(Signature of authorized representative)

Title ....

☆ U. S. GOVERNMENT PRINTING OFFICE : 1941 16—0124—1

1942年12月28日由美国空运指挥部第12空运大队第2航空中队指挥官Duame签发的总第1226号行动命令。命令雷恩机长、鲁宾逊、希克斯三人驾驶序号为651的C-47型运输机完成运输任务，航线从（加纳）阿克拉出发途径（尼日利亚）迈杜古里、（苏丹）喀土穆到达（巴基斯坦）卡拉奇。命令背面附有运输填写的运货单据。

Operation order and invoice to Robert Raine and others, from the Air Corps, War Department.

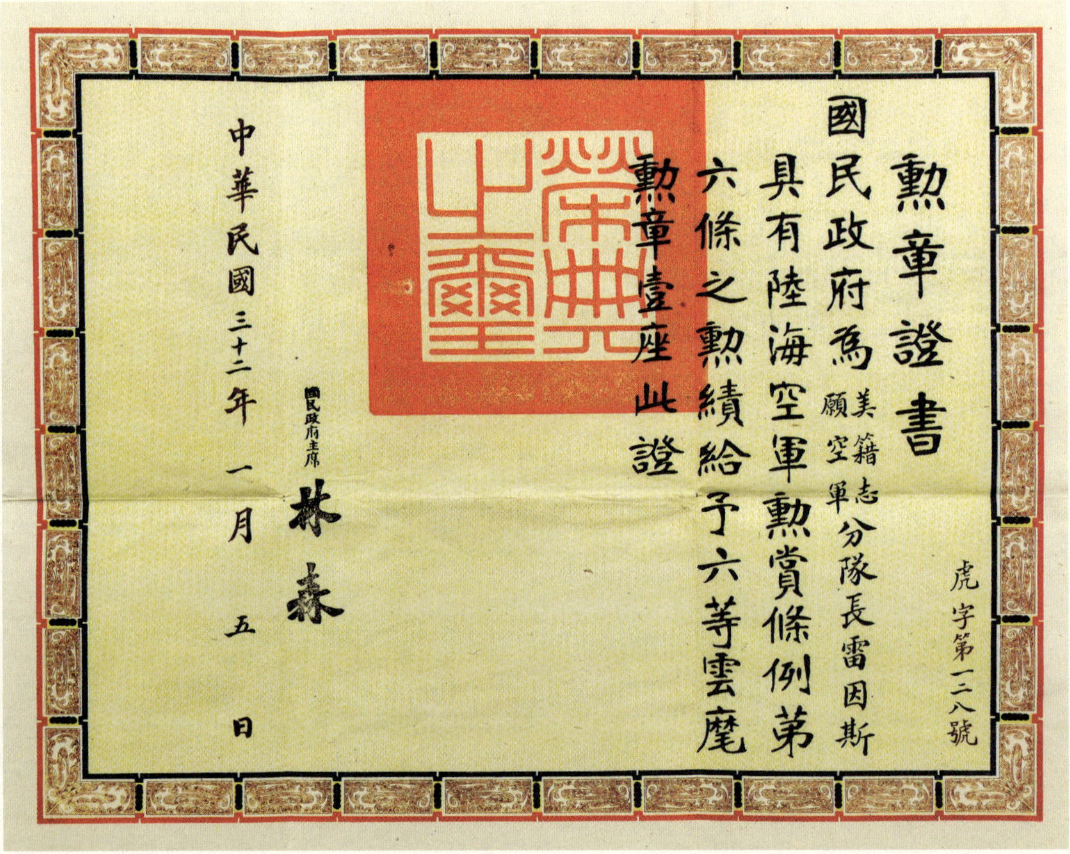

虎字第一二八號

勳章證書

國民政府為美籍志願空軍分隊長雷因斯具有陸海空軍勳賞條例第六條之勳績給予六等雲麾勳章壹座此證

國民政府主席 林森

中華民國三十二年一月五日

由国民政府主席林森1943年1月5日签发的虎字第128号勋章证书，是奖励志愿队分队长雷恩六等云麾勋章的证书。

The certificate issued on January 5th, 1943 with the No. 128 medal of honor by Mr. Lin Sen, then president of KMT government. Raine was awarded 6th grade Cloud and Banner medal of honor.

【背景知识】：云麾勋章系南京国民政府陆海空军勋章之一，因勋章中心刻有云麾而得名。根据1935年6月15日公布的《陆海空军勋赏条例》的规定，凡陆海空军军人，对于国家建有勋绩或“镇摄内乱立有功勋者”，均得颁给云麾勋章。此外，非陆海空军军人或外籍人员对于战事建有勋功者，也可颁给之。将官颁给一至四等，校官颁给三至六等，尉官颁给四至七等，准尉及士官颁给六至九等。

上等官佐由国民政府主席或最高军事长官亲授或派员代授，中等以下官佐及士兵由主管长官或原呈请颁勋机关授予。

名 称	级 别	勋 表
云麾勋章	1（特种大绶）	
	2（大绶）	
	3（黄色大绶）	
	4（特种领绶）	
	5（领绶）	
	6（特种襟绶附勋表）	
	7（襟绶附勋表）	
	8（特种襟绶）	
	9（襟绶）	

陈纳德通知雷恩获勋章的信

Original letter form Claire Lee Chennault

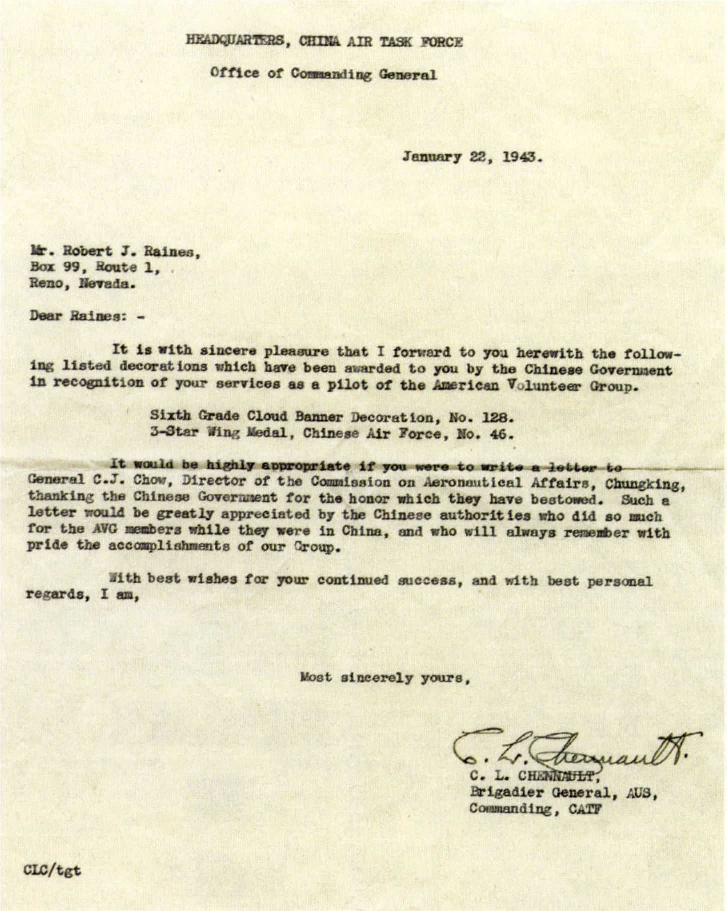

HEADQUARTERS, CHINA AIR TASK FORCE

Office of Commanding General

January 22, 1943.

Mr. Robert J. Raines,
Box 99, Route 1,
Reno, Nevada.

Dear Raines: -

It is with sincere pleasure that I forward to you herewith the following listed decorations which have been awarded to you by the Chinese Government in recognition of your services as a pilot of the American Volunteer Group.

Sixth Grade Cloud Banner Decoration, No. 128.
3-Star Wing Medal, Chinese Air Force, No. 46.

It would be highly appropriate if you were to write a letter to General C.J. Chow, Director of the Commission on Aeronautical Affairs, Chungking, thanking the Chinese Government for the honor which they have bestowed. Such a letter would be greatly appreciated by the Chinese authorities who did so much for the AVG members while they were in China, and who will always remember with pride the accomplishments of our Group.

With best wishes for your continued success, and with best personal regards, I am,

Most sincerely yours,

C. L. Chennault.

C. L. CHENNAULT,
Brigadier General, AUS,
Commanding, CATF

CLC/tgt

Original letter form Claire Lee Chennault, and signed by him to Raine awarding him the medal of honor, dated January 22nd, 1943.

1943年1月22日，陈纳德作为AVG原主管长官亲笔签名通知雷恩，他获得中国政府颁发的编号为128号的六等云麾勋章以及编号为46号的中国空军三星翼章。云麾勋章的编号与勋章证书上编号一致。此时的陈纳德已经为特遣队长官，军衔为准将。信中陈纳德建议雷恩写信给当时在重庆的航空事务委员会主任周志柔，对中国政府颁发的荣誉表示感谢。

要求雷恩参加航空飞行等级考核测试的信件

A letter from War Department to Bartow Army Air Field

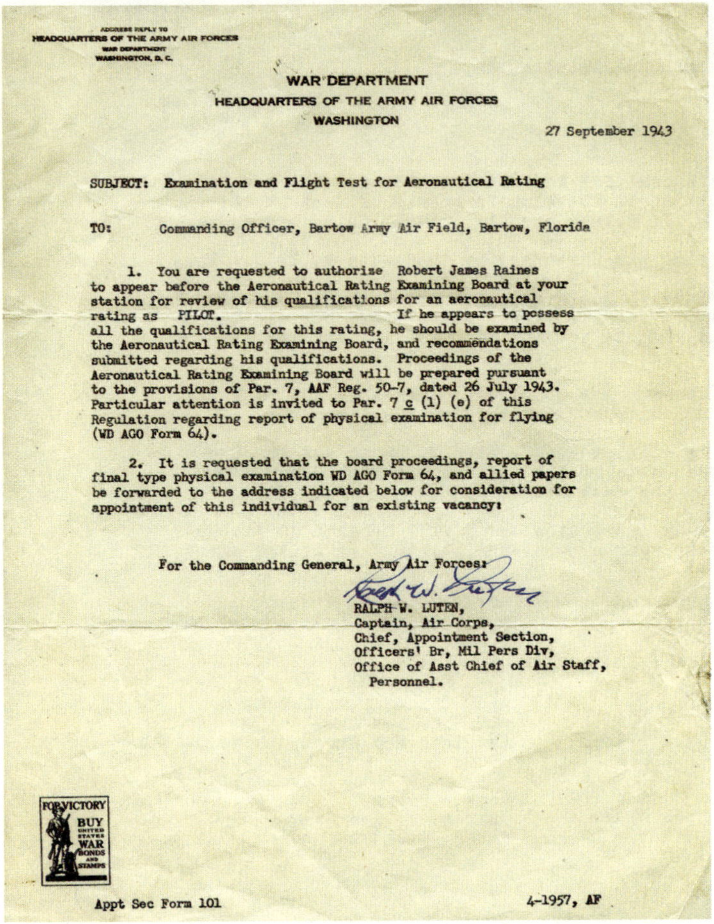

ADDRESS REPLY TO
HEADQUARTERS OF THE ARMY AIR FORCES
WAR DEPARTMENT
WASHINGTON, D. C.

WAR DEPARTMENT
HEADQUARTERS OF THE ARMY AIR FORCES
WASHINGTON

27 September 1943

SUBJECT: Examination and Flight Test for Aeronautical Rating

TO: Commanding Officer, Bartow Army Air Field, Bartow, Florida

1. You are requested to authorize Robert James Raines to appear before the Aeronautical Rating Examining Board at your station for review of his qualifications for an aeronautical rating as PILOT. If he appears to possess all the qualifications for this rating, he should be examined by the Aeronautical Rating Examining Board, and recommendations submitted regarding his qualifications. Proceedings of the Aeronautical Rating Examining Board will be prepared pursuant to the provisions of Par. 7, AAF Reg. 50-7, dated 26 July 1943. Particular attention is invited to Par. 7 c (1) (e) of this Regulation regarding report of physical examination for flying (WD AGO Form 64).

2. It is requested that the board proceedings, report of final type physical examination WD AGO Form 64, and allied papers be forwarded to the address indicated below for consideration for appointment of this individual for an existing vacancy:

For the Commanding General, Army Air Forces:

RALPH W. LUTEN,
Captain, Air Corps,
Chief, Appointment Section,
Officers' Br, Mil Pers Div,
Office of Asst Chief of Air Staff,
Personnel.

FOR VICTORY BUY UNITED STATES WAR BONDS AND STAMPS

Appt Sec Form 101 4-1957, AF

信件是美国陆军航空队长官拉尔夫LUTEN 1943年9月27日签发给福罗里达州巴托空军基地的长官的。要求雷恩到航空评级站进行航空飞行等级考核测试，如果具备相应等级，评级审查委员将推荐、提交其资格。评级审查委员会将依据1943年7月26日有关规定的条款第7段50−7条7c（1）、（e）进行飞行体检。董事会将出具体检的最终报告，并将报告转发至盟军处，再根据现有职位空缺进行任命。

A letter from War Department to Bartow Army Air Field, Bartow, Florida to authorize R. J. Raine for review of his qualifications for an aeronautical rating as pilot, September 27th 1943.

代表雷恩的私人信件

A letter from Chauncey H. Laughlin

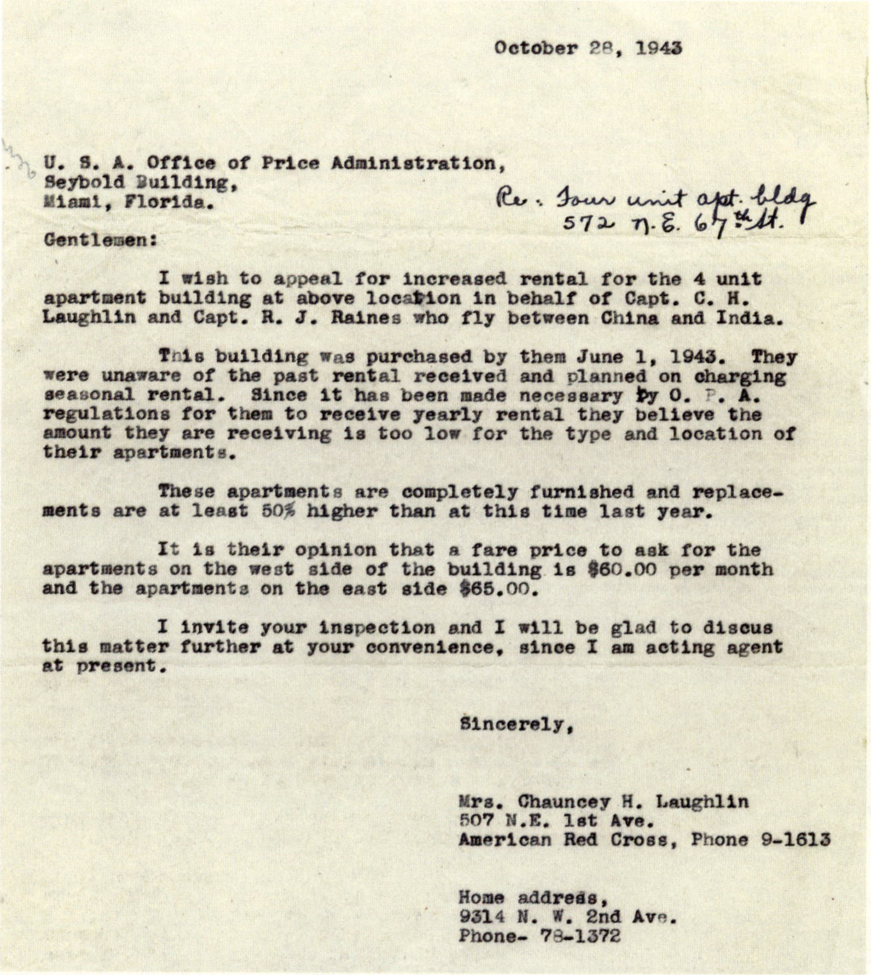

October 28, 1943

U. S. A. Office of Price Administration,
Seybold Building,
Miami, Florida.

Re. Four unit apt. bldg
572 N.E. 67th St.

Gentlemen:

I wish to appeal for increased rental for the 4 unit apartment building at above location in behalf of Capt. C. H. Laughlin and Capt. R. J. Raines who fly between China and India.

This building was purchased by them June 1, 1943. They were unaware of the past rental received and planned on charging seasonal rental. Since it has been made necessary by O. P. A. regulations for them to receive yearly rental they believe the amount they are receiving is too low for the type and location of their apartments.

These apartments are completely furnished and replacements are at least 50% higher than at this time last year.

It is their opinion that a fare price to ask for the apartments on the west side of the building is $60.00 per month and the apartments on the east side $65.00.

I invite your inspection and I will be glad to discus this matter further at your convenience, since I am acting agent at present.

Sincerely,

Mrs. Chauncey H. Laughlin
507 N.E. 1st Ave.
American Red Cross, Phone 9-1613

Home address,
9314 N. W. 2nd Ave.
Phone- 78-1372

1943年10月28日美国红十字会劳克林女士代表雷恩写给美国价格管理办公室的，要求价格管理办公室提高劳克林女士和雷恩1943年6月1日购买的四套公寓的租金。信中提到雷恩是机长，往返于印度和中国之间。

Letter from CNAC to Deputy Commissioner of Police testifying for Raine's competency to hold a shotgun license.

中航公司替雷恩申请持枪的信件

A letter from CNAC

Letter for request for Raine to Calcutta Police Headquarters for a license covering one 12 gauge automatic shot gun from CNAC, December 9th, 1943.

1943年12月9日中国航空公司业务经理夏普为雷恩向加尔各答警察总署、武器部申请持枪。信上说雷恩讲信用，守纪律，喜爱运动，钟情打猎，特申请持有编号为60388，12发自动猎枪及持有编号为65431的405型温彻斯特步枪执照。

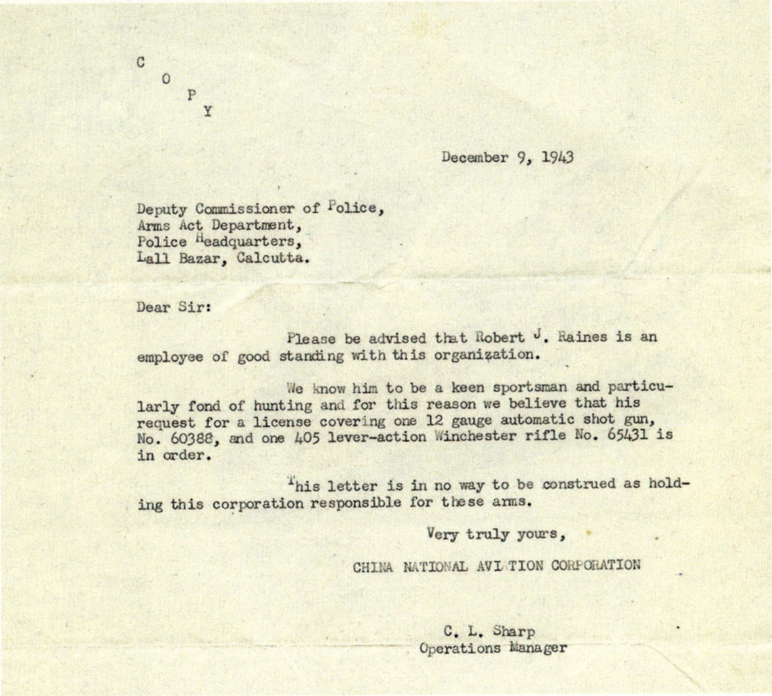

C O P Y

December 9, 1943

Deputy Commissioner of Police,
Arms Act Department,
Police Headquarters,
Lall Bazar, Calcutta.

Dear Sir:

Please be advised that Robert J. Raines is an employee of good standing with this organization.

We know him to be a keen sportsman and particularly fond of hunting and for this reason we believe that his request for a license covering one 12 gauge automatic shot gun, No. 60388, and one 405 lever-action Winchester rifle No. 65431 is in order.

This letter is in no way to be construed as holding this corporation responsible for these arms.

Very truly yours,

CHINA NATIONAL AVI TION CORPORATION

C. L. Sharp
Operations Manager

1943年介绍雷恩的剪报

Newspaper cutting on Raine in 1943

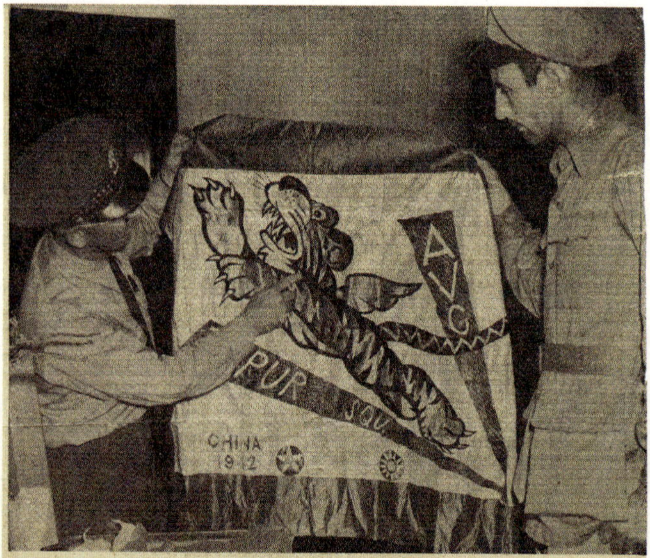

FLYING TIGER BANNER is displayed by Robert Raines (right) of Reno, Nev., for the scrutiny of Customs Inspector Farrell Crawford. Former pilot with the AVG in China, Gaines now is a ferry pilot for China National Aviation corp.

Flying Tiger, Bored, May Join Marines For Action

A former "Flying Tiger" who bagged at least six Japanese planes, is getting bored with handling transports over the mountainous Chinese-Indian route, and may join the Marines to get back into sky combat.

Robert Raines, of Reno, Nev., told about his dilemma Thursday in Miami upon returning to the United States aboard a Pan American transatlantic clipper to recuperate from an attack of malaria. He now is a pilot for the China National Aviation corp., flying cargo and soldiers over the route from India to China.

"They treat me mighty well out there, and I may go back," he said. "But it's boring. I haven't seen a Jap plane since I joined up with CNAC last August, although some have been reported along the route, and I flew one day through an alert.

MAY JOIN MARINES

"I have about decided to join the Marines, though. I'm getting tired of flying transport planes."

If he does seek a Marine commission, he'll have the backing of a recommendation from Maj. Gen. Claire Chennault, who led the Flying Tigers of the American Volunteer Group through a highly successful campaign against the Japs in China and Burma. The general passed through Miami Wednesday on his way to Washington.

Raines joined the AVG in August, 1941, but didn't get into combat until April, 1942, because he was kept busy on other assignments.

He was one of the pilots who went to Africa to return the first group of P-40 fighter planes provided by the government.

Between April and July, however, he saw plenty of action. He was officially credited with downing six planes, and had nine other "probables."

He brought with him the scroll given him by grateful citizens of Hengyang, China, because he and two other Flying Tigers tackled a group of 24 fighter planes over the city and shot down six of them.

【全文翻译】：

内华达州里诺市的罗伯特·雷恩（右）将飞虎队（AVG）旗帜向海关检查员发内尔·格劳夫展示，并接受检查。

飞虎队员深感枯燥，欲加入海军陆战队战斗

至少击毁6架日军敌机的前飞虎队员对于中印驼峰航线的运输任务感到枯燥乏味。他希望加入海军陆战队，以期重返空中战场。

内华达州里诺市的罗伯特·雷恩为了疟疾后的康复疗养，周四在迈阿密搭乘跨大西洋客轮返回美国。他现任中国航空公司飞行员，往返在中印航线间运输货物和兵员。

"他们把我治好后我还将再次回去，"他说，"那里真是很枯燥乏味，我从去年8月加入中航公司以来，再没见过一架日军飞机。尽管我每次飞行的时候都会接到一条关于日军飞机在航线附近出没的报告。"

"所以我决心参加海军陆战队，我对驾驶运输机真的感到乏味。"如果他对海军陆战队委员会提出请求，他将会得到克莱尔·陈纳德将军的推荐。陈纳德将军是领导美国志愿队在中国和缅甸自始至终成功打击日军的致胜者。陈纳德将军周三经过迈阿密去往华盛顿。

雷恩于1941年8月参加美国志愿队，因为忙于执行其他任务，一直没有投入战斗，直到1942年4月。

他是在非洲地区第一批驾驶由政府提供的P-40战斗机返航的人员。

在四月至七月间，他多次驾机参战，被正式宣布击落的敌机达6架，但事实上还有其他9架也可能被击落。

他带来了一本中国衡阳市民向他表示感激之情的签名册。因为他和其他飞虎队员在衡阳上空阻绝了24架来犯敌机机群，并击落了其中的6架。

孟加拉政府关于雷恩武器许可证的函件

Letter or inquiry from Government of Bengal to CNAC on Raine's arms

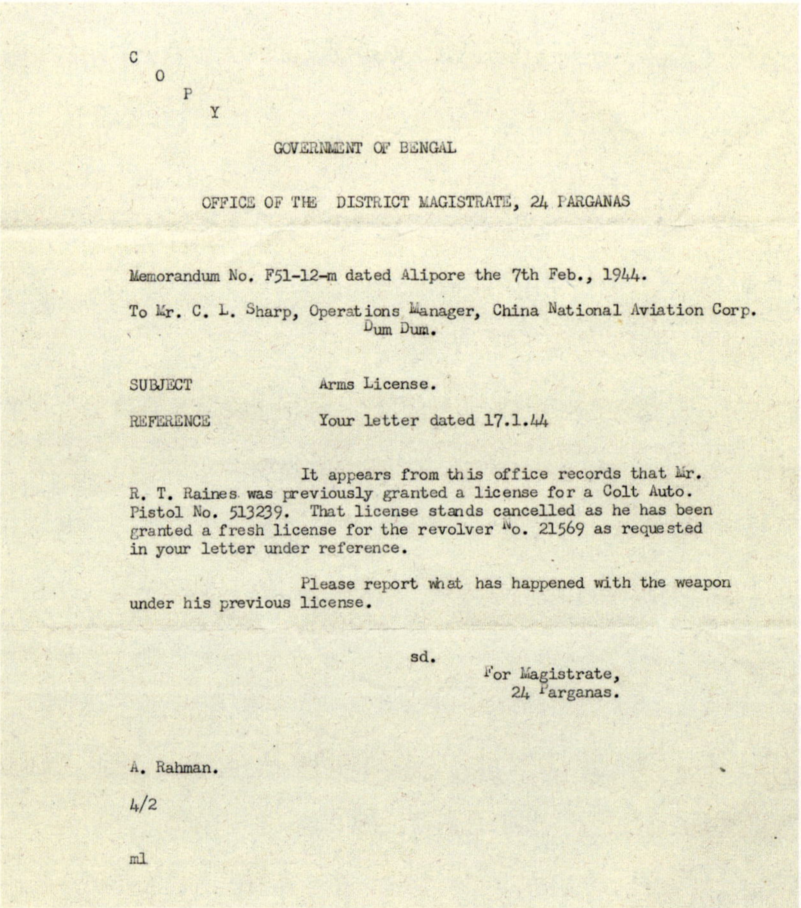

C
O
P
Y

GOVERNMENT OF BENGAL

OFFICE OF THE DISTRICT MAGISTRATE, 24 PARGANAS

Memorandum No. F51-12-m dated Alipore the 7th Feb., 1944.

To Mr. C. L. Sharp, Operations Manager, China National Aviation Corp.
Dum Dum.

SUBJECT Arms License.

REFERENCE Your letter dated 17.1.44

It appears from this office records that Mr. R. T. Raines was previously granted a license for a Colt Auto. Pistol No. 513239. That license stands cancelled as he has been granted a fresh license for the revolver No. 21569 as requested in your letter under reference.

Please report what has happened with the weapon under his previous license.

sd.
For Magistrate,
24 Parganas.

A. Rahman.

4/2

ml

Letter or inquiry from Government of Bengal to CNAC on Raine's arms, Feb 7th, 1944.

1944年1月17日，中国航空公司业务经理夏普先生，曾为雷恩的武器携带许可问题向孟加拉政府提出申请，该函件是孟加拉政府对申请的回复。回复的日期为1944年2月7日，函件备忘录编号为N0.F51－12－M。函件中提到：从上报的记录显示，雷恩以前有枪号为513239的持枪证，一旦新的编号为21569的左轮手枪持枪证生效，以前的持枪证立即失效，并要求告知雷恩以前的持枪证发放的时间。

雷恩在孟加拉收据两张
Two receipts

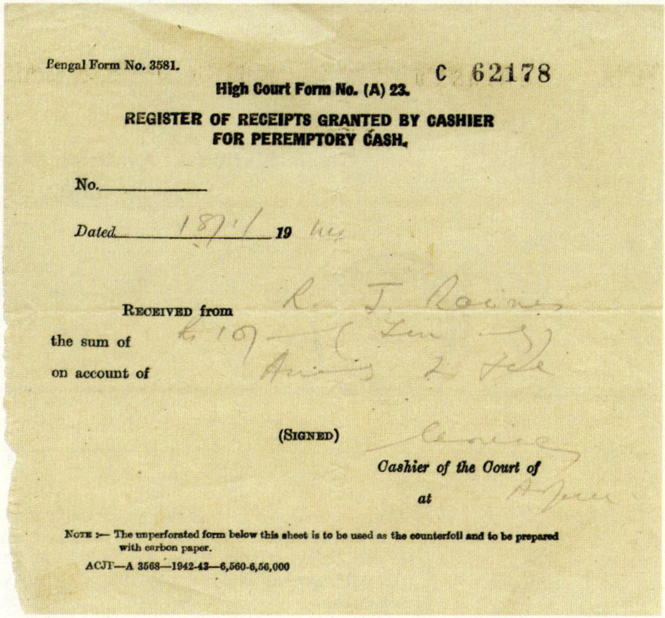

Bengal Form No. 3581.

C 62178

High Court Form No. (A) 23.

REGISTER OF RECEIPTS GRANTED BY CASHIER FOR PEREMPTORY CASH.

No.____________

Dated 18/1/ 19 44

RECEIVED from R. J. Raines

the sum of

on account of

(SIGNED)

Cashier of the Court of

at

NOTE :— The unperforated form below this sheet is to be used as the counterfoil and to be prepared with carbon paper.

ACJT—A 3568—1942-43—6,560-6,56,000

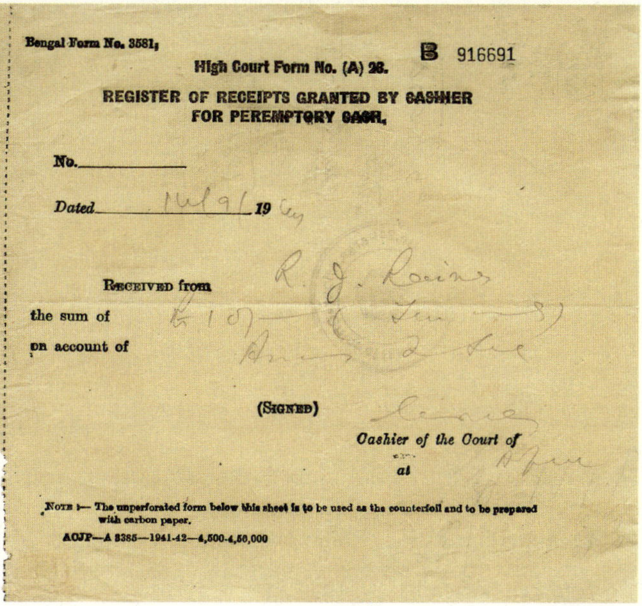

Bengal Form No. 3581.

B 916691

High Court Form No. (A) 23.

REGISTER OF RECEIPTS GRANTED BY CASHIER FOR PEREMPTORY CASH.

No.____________

Dated 14/9/ 19 44

RECEIVED from R. J. Raines

the sum of

on account of

(SIGNED)

Cashier of the Court of

at

NOTE :— The unperforated form below this sheet is to be used as the counterfoil and to be prepared with carbon paper.

ACJP—A 3385—1941-42—4,500-4,56,000

编号C62178和编号B916691的孟加拉收据，均用铅笔填写单据。单据上雷恩的名字清晰可辨。单据填写日期分别为1944年1月18日和9月14日。单据上还盖有圆形淡蓝色印章。

Two receipts issued by Bengal high court for Raine on peremptory cash payment.

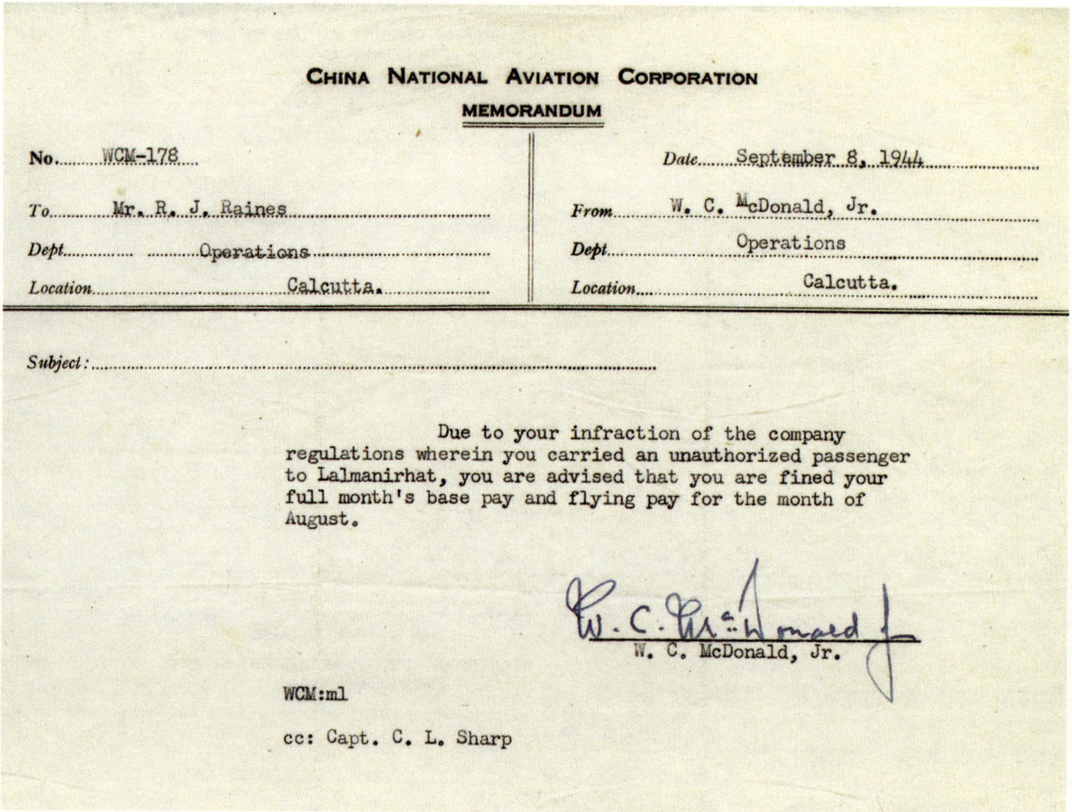

CHINA NATIONAL AVIATION CORPORATION

MEMORANDUM

No. WCM-178

Date September 8, 1944

To Mr. R. J. Raines

From W. C. McDonald, Jr.

Dept Operations

Dept Operations

Location Calcutta.

Location Calcutta.

Subject:

Due to your infraction of the company regulations wherein you carried an unauthorized passenger to Lalmanirhat, you are advised that you are fined your full month's base pay and flying pay for the month of August.

W. C. McDonald, Jr.

W. C. McDonald, Jr.

WCM:ml

cc: Capt. C. L. Sharp

1944年9月8日，中国航空公司致雷恩的处罚记录，由麦克唐纳先生签署。当时雷恩在印度东北部城市加尔各答。内容是关于惩罚雷恩违反中国航空公司的规定，运送一名未经许可的乘客到（孟加拉）Lalmanirhat，因此被公司处罚，扣罚8月份的月基本工资和飞行补贴。

A Memorandum to R.J. Raine on unauthorized passenger carrying from China National Aviation Corporation, September 8th, 1944.

M. Scharman申请参加美国海军预备役的信

Two Letters from M. Scharman

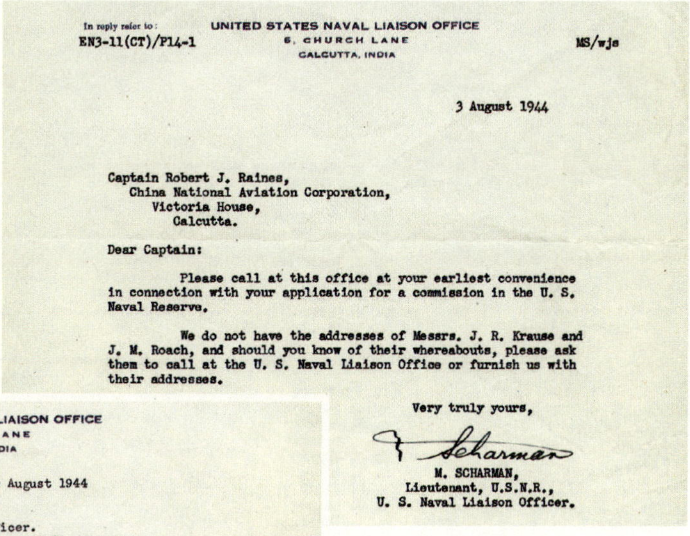

In reply refer to:
EN3-11(CT)/P14-1

UNITED STATES NAVAL LIAISON OFFICE
6, CHURCH LANE
CALCUTTA, INDIA

MS/wjs

3 August 1944

Captain Robert J. Raines,
China National Aviation Corporation,
Victoria House,
Calcutta.

Dear Captain:

Please call at this office at your earliest convenience in connection with your application for a commission in the U. S. Naval Reserve.

We do not have the addresses of Messrs. J. R. Krause and J. M. Roach, and should you know of their whereabouts, please ask them to call at the U. S. Naval Liaison Office or furnish us with their addresses.

Very truly yours,

M. Scharman

M. SCHARMAN,
Lieutenant, U.S.N.R.,
U. S. Naval Liaison Officer.

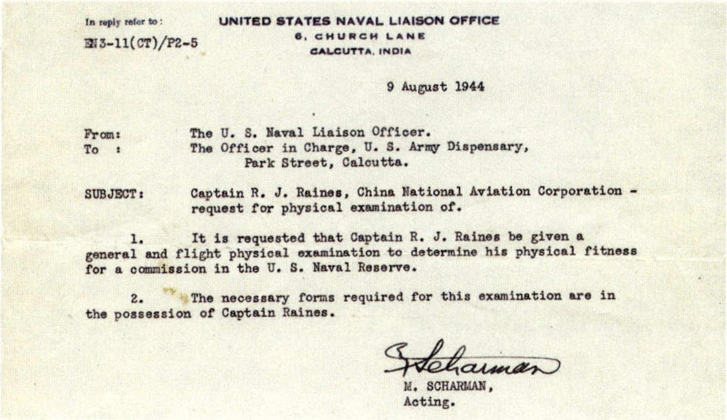

In reply refer to:
EN3-11(CT)/P2-5

UNITED STATES NAVAL LIAISON OFFICE
6, CHURCH LANE
CALCUTTA, INDIA

9 August 1944

From: The U. S. Naval Liaison Officer.
To : The Officer in Charge, U. S. Army Dispensary,
Park Street, Calcutta.

SUBJECT: Captain R. J. Raines, China National Aviation Corporation - request for physical examination of.

1. It is requested that Captain R. J. Raines be given a general and flight physical examination to determine his physical fitness for a commission in the U. S. Naval Reserve.

2. The necessary forms required for this examination are in the possession of Captain Raines.

M. Scharman

M. SCHARMAN,
Acting.

1944年8月3日，由美国海军联络处给中国航空公司的机长雷恩致函，请他尽早就参加美国海军预备役一事致电联络处。同时，联络处请求雷恩转告或者提供克劳斯和洛奇先生的地址。另有一封函件是1944年8月9日美国海军联络处再次致雷恩的函，内容涉及雷恩参加海军预备役前进行体格检查的相关事宜。两份函件均由美国海军联络处上尉Scharman签署。

Two Letters to Captain Robert Raine from M. Scharman, US Naval Liaison Officer, regarding his application for US Naval Reserve, August 3rd, 1944.

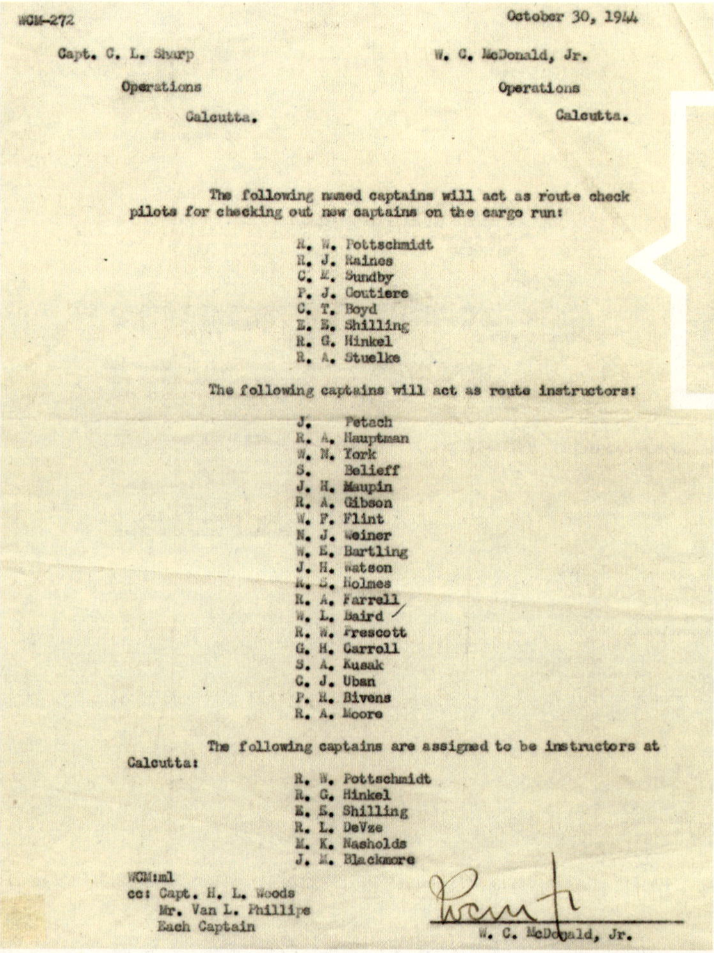

WCM-272 October 30, 1944

Capt. C. L. Sharp W. C. McDonald, Jr.
Operations Operations
Calcutta. Calcutta.

The following named captains will act as route check pilots for checking out new captains on the cargo run:

R. W. Pottschmidt
R. J. Raines
C. E. Sundby
P. J. Coutiere
C. T. Boyd
E. E. Shilling
R. G. Hinkel
R. A. Stuelke

The following captains will act as route instructors:

J. Petach
R. A. Hauptman
W. N. York
S. Belieff
J. H. Maupin
R. A. Gibson
W. F. Flint
N. J. Weiner
W. E. Bartling
J. H. Watson
R. S. Holmes
R. A. Farrell
W. L. Baird
R. W. Prescott
G. H. Carroll
S. A. Kusak
C. J. Uban
P. H. Bivens
R. A. Moore

The following captains are assigned to be instructors at Calcutta:

R. W. Pottschmidt
R. G. Hinkel
E. E. Shilling
R. L. DeVze
M. K. Nasholds
J. M. Blackmore

WCM:ml
cc: Capt. H. L. Woods
Mr. Van L. Phillips
Each Captain

W. C. McDonald, Jr.

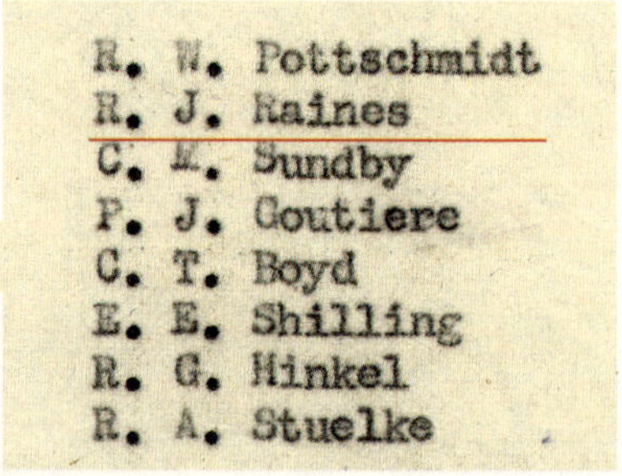

R. W. Pottschmidt
R. J. Raines
C. E. Sundby
P. J. Coutiere
C. T. Boyd
E. E. Shilling
R. G. Hinkel
R. A. Stuelke

1944年10月30日，中国航空公司驻印度加尔各答的飞行员名单，名单中有飞行员33名，分为三组，分工明确。一组8名飞行员，在货物运输航线上负责航路查核，雷恩名列其中；二组19名飞行员，负责航路指导；三组6名飞行员，分配在加尔各答担任教员。此名单由麦克唐纳先生签署。

Lists of route check pilots, route instructors and instructors, October 30th, 1944.

保险公司回复雷恩购买养老保险的信件

Letter from Sun Life Assurance Company

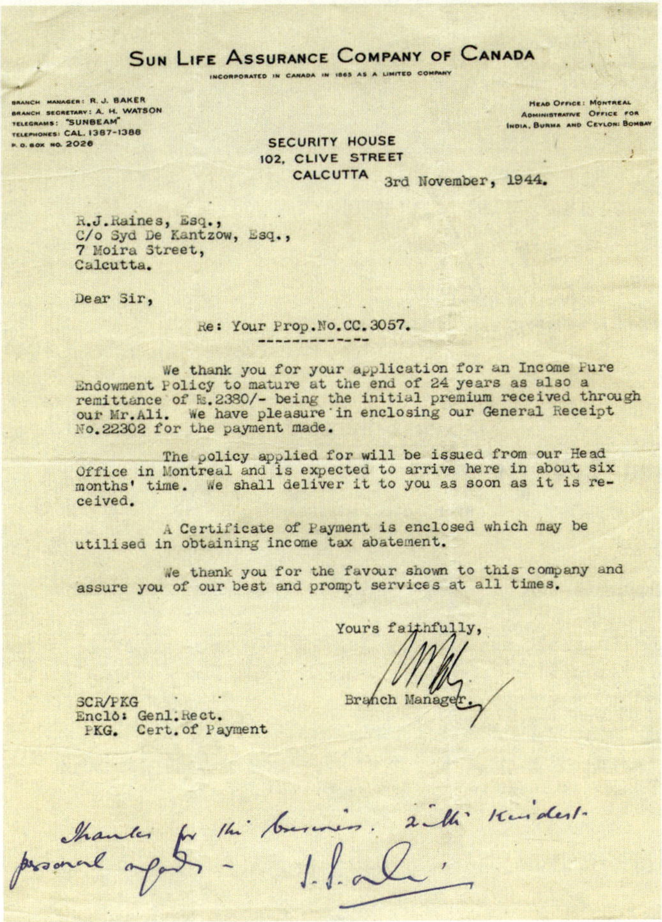

SUN LIFE ASSURANCE COMPANY OF CANADA

INCORPORATED IN CANADA IN 1865 AS A LIMITED COMPANY

BRANCH MANAGER: R. J. BAKER
BRANCH SECRETARY: A. H. WATSON
TELEGRAMS: "SUNBEAM"
TELEPHONES: CAL. 1387-1388
P. O. BOX NO. 2026

HEAD OFFICE: MONTREAL
ADMINISTRATIVE OFFICE FOR
INDIA, BURMA AND CEYLON: BOMBAY

SECURITY HOUSE
102, CLIVE STREET
CALCUTTA

3rd November, 1944.

R.J.Raines, Esq.,
C/o Syd De Kantzow, Esq.,
7 Moira Street,
Calcutta.

Dear Sir,

Re: Your Prop.No.CC.3057.

We thank you for your application for an Income Pure Endowment Policy to mature at the end of 24 years as also a remittance of Rs.2380/- being the initial premium received through our Mr.Ali. We have pleasure in enclosing our General Receipt No.22302 for the payment made.

The policy applied for will be issued from our Head Office in Montreal and is expected to arrive here in about six months' time. We shall deliver it to you as soon as it is received.

A Certificate of Payment is enclosed which may be utilised in obtaining income tax abatement.

We thank you for the favour shown to this company and assure you of our best and prompt services at all times.

Yours faithfully,

Branch Manager.

SCR/PKG
Enclô: Genl.Rect.
PKG. Cert.of Payment

Thanks for the business. With kindest personal regards –

1944年11月3日，从加拿大阳光人寿保险公司给雷恩的信件可以看出，雷恩购买的养老保险已经支付了预付款 2380 卢比，阳光人寿保险公司的阿里先生经办此事，收款收据编号为22302，交给雷恩。保险单则因为阳光保险公司的本部位于蒙特利尔，最终到达加尔各答需要大约六个月的时间才能交付雷恩本人。保险公司告知雷恩保险的付款凭证可以用来减免税收。信中还感谢雷恩并承诺在保险期间将提供优质满意的服务，信件由分公司经理签署。

Letter on Raine’s Policy from Sun Life Assurance Company of Canada.

雷恩保险公司保险支付证明及收据

Two receipts

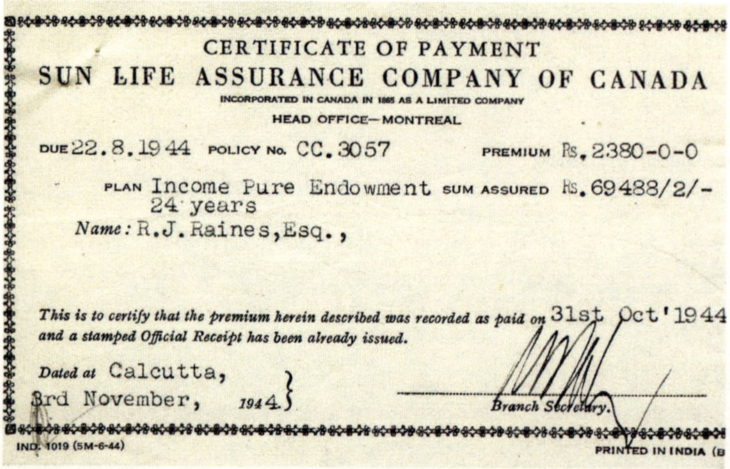

CERTIFICATE OF PAYMENT

SUN LIFE ASSURANCE COMPANY OF CANADA

INCORPORATED IN CANADA IN 1865 AS A LIMITED COMPANY

HEAD OFFICE—MONTREAL

DUE 22.8.1944 POLICY No. CC.3057 PREMIUM Rs.2380-0-0

PLAN Income Pure Endowment 24 years SUM ASSURED Rs.69488/2/-

Name: R.J.Raines,Esq.,

This is to certify that the premium herein described was recorded as paid on 31st Oct'1944 *and a stamped Official Receipt has been already issued.*

Dated at Calcutta, 3rd November, *1944*

Branch Secretary.

IND. 1019 (5M-6-44) PRINTED IN INDIA (B

Two receipts, November 3, 1944.

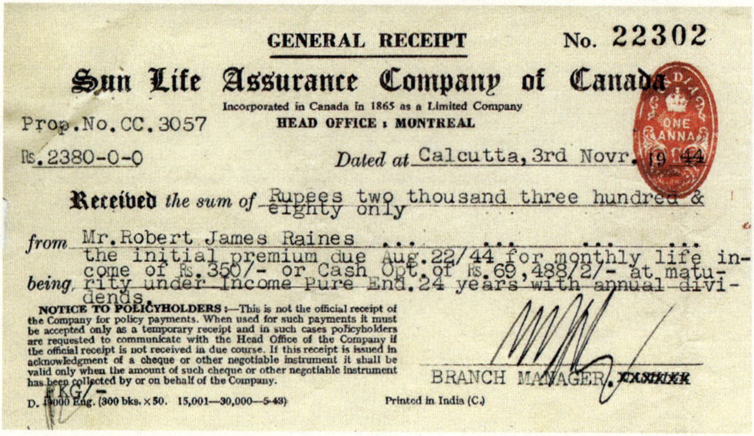

GENERAL RECEIPT No. 22302

Sun Life Assurance Company of Canada

Incorporated in Canada in 1865 as a Limited Company

HEAD OFFICE : MONTREAL

Prop.No.CC.3057

Rs.2380-0-0

Dated at Calcutta,3rd Novr. 19 44

ONE ANNA

Received *the sum of* Rupees two thousand three hundred & eighty only

from Mr.Robert James Raines ... ...

being the initial premium due Aug.22/44 for monthly life income of Rs.350/- or Cash Opt.of Rs.69,488/2/- at maturity under Income Pure End.24 years with annual dividends.

NOTICE TO POLICYHOLDERS :—This is not the official receipt of the Company for policy payments. When used for such payments it must be accepted only as a temporary receipt and in such cases policyholders are requested to communicate with the Head Office of the Company if the official receipt is not received in due course. If this receipt is issued in acknowledgment of a cheque or other negotiable instrument it shall be valid only when the amount of such cheque or other negotiable instrument has been collected by or on behalf of the Company.

KG/-

BRANCH MANAGER.

D. 4000 Eng. (300 bks. × 50. 15,001—30,000—5-43) Printed in India (C.)

雷恩购买人寿养老保险的支付证明及收据，日期为1944年11月3日。保险收据单号为22302，与加拿大阳光保险公司给雷恩信件上的日期、内容、金额均相符合。雷恩的保险编号为CC.3057，保险费预付款金额为2380卢比，保险费每月分期付款金额为350卢比，保险期限24年，到期可获得69488卢比的保险收益。支付证明及收据均由分公司经理签署，签署地点为加尔各答。

香港政府给雷恩的收据

Receipt from Hong Kong Government

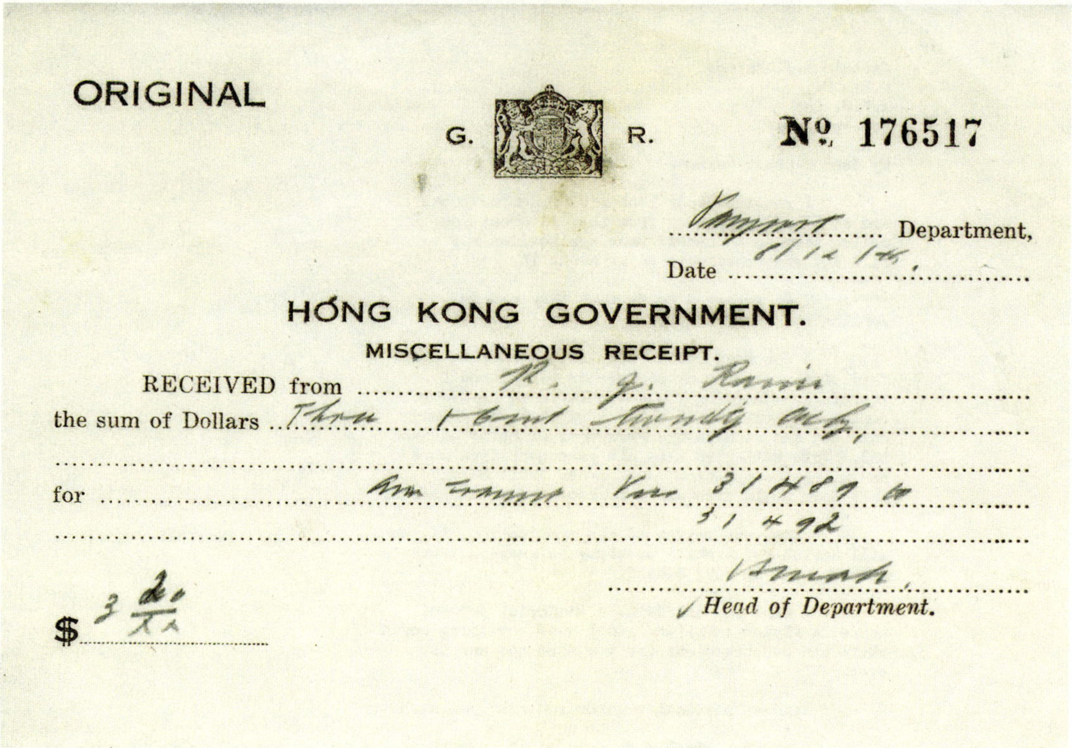

ORIGINAL

G. R. №. 176517

Passport Department,

Date 6/12/44.

HONG KONG GOVERNMENT.

MISCELLANEOUS RECEIPT.

RECEIVED from R. J. Raine

the sum of Dollars Three ...

for ... 31489 to 31492

Head of Department.

$ 3 20/xx

香港政府给雷恩的收据，日期为1944年12月6日。收据编号为176517。正文部分用铅笔填写，雷恩的名字清晰可辨，金额为3.2美元，其他字迹模糊，难以辨识。

Receipt for Raine from Hong Kong Government.

美国参议员派特麦卡伦给雷恩的回信

A letter from Pat McCarran

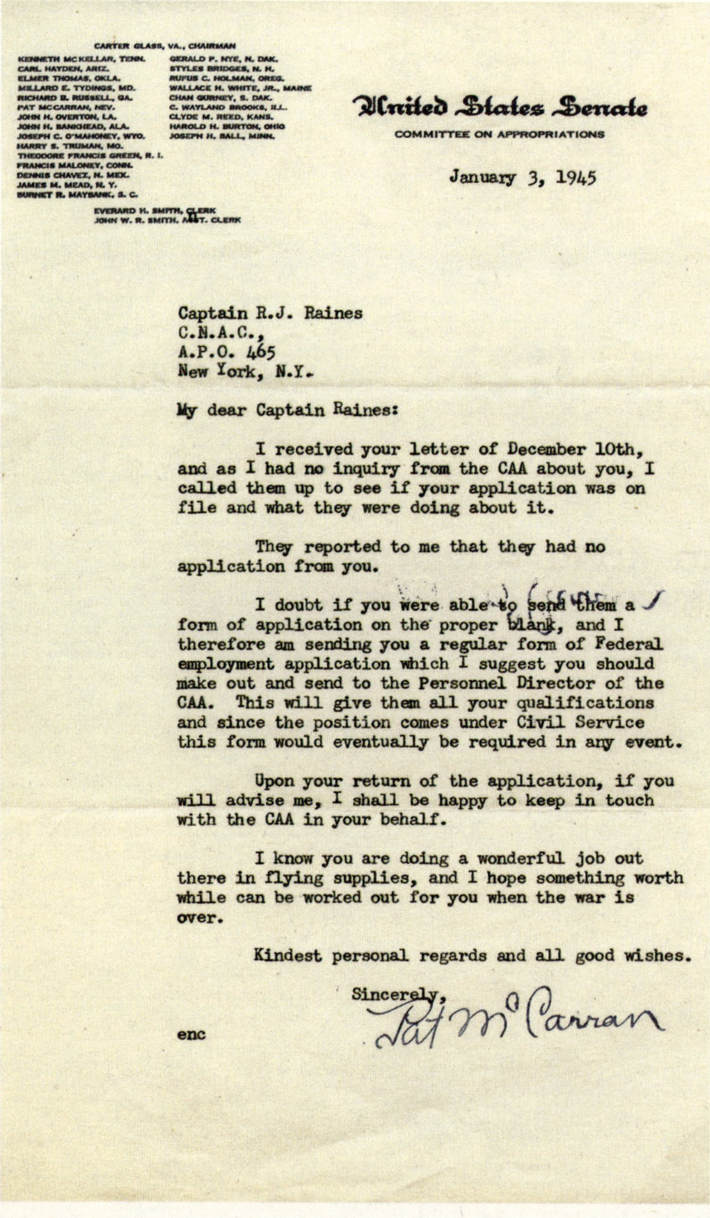

CARTER GLASS, VA., CHAIRMAN

KENNETH MCKELLAR, TENN.
CARL HAYDEN, ARIZ.
ELMER THOMAS, OKLA.
MILLARD E. TYDINGS, MD.
RICHARD B. RUSSELL, GA.
PAT MCCARRAN, NEV.
JOHN H. OVERTON, LA.
JOHN H. BANKHEAD, ALA.
JOSEPH C. O'MAHONEY, WYO.
HARRY S. TRUMAN, MO.
THEODORE FRANCIS GREEN, R. I.
FRANCIS MALONEY, CONN.
DENNIS CHAVEZ, N. MEX.
JAMES M. MEAD, N. Y.
BURNET R. MAYBANK, S. C.

GERALD P. NYE, N. DAK.
STYLES BRIDGES, N. H.
RUFUS C. HOLMAN, OREG.
WALLACE H. WHITE, JR., MAINE
CHAN GURNEY, S. DAK.
C. WAYLAND BROOKS, ILL.
CLYDE M. REED, KANS.
HAROLD H. BURTON, OHIO
JOSEPH H. BALL, MINN.

EVERARD H. SMITH, CLERK
JOHN W. R. SMITH, ASST. CLERK

United States Senate
COMMITTEE ON APPROPRIATIONS

January 3, 1945

Captain R.J. Raines
C.N.A.C.,
A.P.O. 465
New York, N.Y.

My dear Captain Raines:

I received your letter of December 10th, and as I had no inquiry from the CAA about you, I called them up to see if your application was on file and what they were doing about it.

They reported to me that they had no application from you.

I doubt if you were able to send them a form of application on the proper blank, and I therefore am sending you a regular form of Federal employment application which I suggest you should make out and send to the Personnel Director of the CAA. This will give them all your qualifications and since the position comes under Civil Service this form would eventually be required in any event.

Upon your return of the application, if you will advise me, I shall be happy to keep in touch with the CAA in your behalf.

I know you are doing a wonderful job out there in flying supplies, and I hope something worth while can be worked out for you when the war is over.

Kindest personal regards and all good wishes.

Sincerely,

Pat McCarran

enc

1945年1月3日，美国参议员派特麦卡伦给雷恩的回信，告知雷恩寄给他的信件已经收到，经派特麦卡伦查询，在CAA（美国民航管理局）没有找到雷恩申报的申请。他建议雷恩做一份正规的就业申请表，提供雷恩履职以来的履历资料，并将它送交CAA的人事主任，并表示他将竭力为雷恩在CAA申请职位提供应有的帮助。在信中，派特麦卡伦还高度赞扬雷恩在飞行运输工作中取得的成就，并希望他战后早日归来并且解决好在CAA申请职位的事宜。

A letter from US Senator Pat McCarran to Captain R. J. Raine, January 3rd, 1945.

中国航空公司对雷恩表彰函

CNAC commendation to Raine

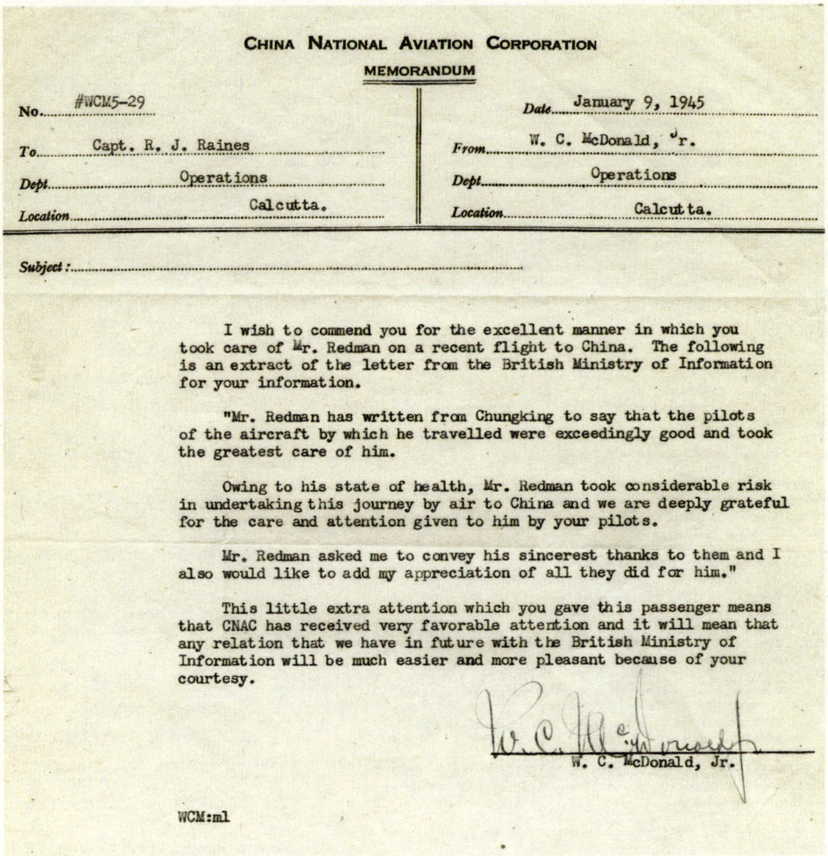

CHINA NATIONAL AVIATION CORPORATION

MEMORANDUM

No. #WCM5-29
Date January 9, 1945

To Capt. R. J. Raines
From W. C. McDonald, Jr.

Dept Operations
Dept Operations

Location Calcutta.
Location Calcutta.

Subject :

I wish to commend you for the excellent manner in which you took care of Mr. Redman on a recent flight to China. The following is an extract of the letter from the British Ministry of Information for your information.

"Mr. Redman has written from Chungking to say that the pilots of the aircraft by which he travelled were exceedingly good and took the greatest care of him.

Owing to his state of health, Mr. Redman took considerable risk in undertaking this journey by air to China and we are deeply grateful for the care and attention given to him by your pilots.

Mr. Redman asked me to convey his sincerest thanks to them and I also would like to add my appreciation of all they did for him."

This little extra attention which you gave this passenger means that CNAC has received very favorable attention and it will mean that any relation that we have in future with the British Ministry of Information will be much easier and more pleasant because of your courtesy.

W. C. McDonald, Jr.

WCM:ml

1945年1月9日，中国航空公司麦克唐纳先生签署，地点在加尔各答。内容为表彰雷恩在最近飞往中国的航线上对英国信息部雷德曼先生无微不至的照顾。雷德曼先生从重庆来信感谢雷恩机组成员对他的关怀和照顾，并请麦克唐纳先生向雷恩机组转达诚挚的谢意。麦克唐纳先生也认为雷恩机组受到雷德曼关注和感谢，对中国航空公司的肯定，有利于今后中国航空公司和英国信息部加强协作关系。

CNAC commendation to Raine, January 9th, 1945.

中国银行纽约分行给雷恩的信件

A Letter from Bank of China New York Agency

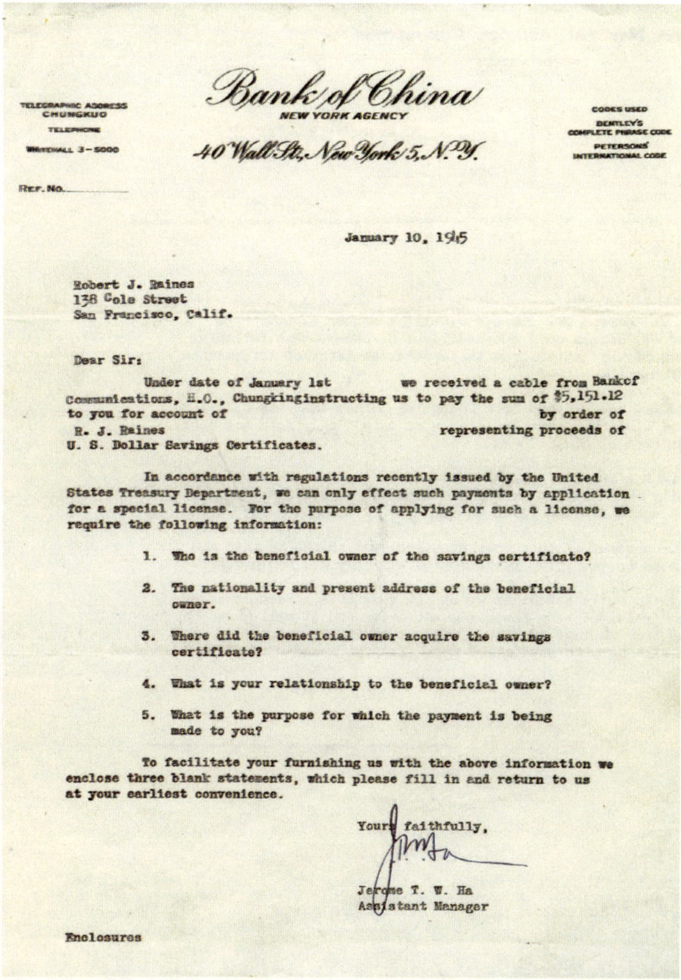

Bank of China
NEW YORK AGENCY
40 Wall St., New York 5, N.Y.

TELEGRAPHIC ADDRESS
CHUNGKUO
TELEPHONE
WHITEHALL 3-5000

CODES USED
BENTLEY'S
COMPLETE PHRASE CODE
PETERSONS'
INTERNATIONAL CODE

REF. NO.

January 10, 1945

Robert J. Raines
138 Cole Street
San Francisco, Calif.

Dear Sir:

Under date of January 1st we received a cable from Bankof Communications, H.O., Chungkinginstructing us to pay the sum of $5,151.12 to you for account of by order of R. J. Raines representing proceeds of U. S. Dollar Savings Certificates.

In accordance with regulations recently issued by the United States Treasury Department, we can only effect such payments by application for a special license. For the purpose of applying for such a license, we require the following information:

1. Who is the beneficial owner of the savings certificate?
2. The nationality and present address of the beneficial owner.
3. Where did the beneficial owner acquire the savings certificate?
4. What is your relationship to the beneficial owner?
5. What is the purpose for which the payment is being made to you?

To facilitate your furnishing us with the above information we enclose three blank statements, which please fill in and return to us at your earliest convenience.

Yours faithfully,

Jerome T. W. Ha
Assistant Manager

Enclosures

A Letter from Bank of China New York Agency informing Raine receiving a sum of US $5,151.12 from Bank of Communications, Chung King, China.

1945年1月10日，中国银行纽约分行副经理杰罗姆先生以信件方式告知雷恩：收到中国银行重庆分行发来的电报，需向雷恩支付5151.12美元。但是依据美国财政部最近发布的相关规定，支付这笔款项必须申请一个特别的许可证，并需要雷恩补充信中提及的5条信息资料给中国银行才能如愿申请。5条需要雷恩明确的资料如下：谁是储蓄金的受益人？受益人的国籍和目前的地址？受益人获取储蓄金的具体地点？雷恩和受益人的关系？这笔钱的用途有何打算等等。为了方便雷恩提供以上资料，中国银行提供了三份空白表给雷恩，并请他填好后尽快返还给中国银行办理随后的业务工作。当时雷恩的收件地址是加利福尼亚州日金山科尔大街138号。

雷恩家人给中国银行纽约分行的回信

A letter from William St. Clair

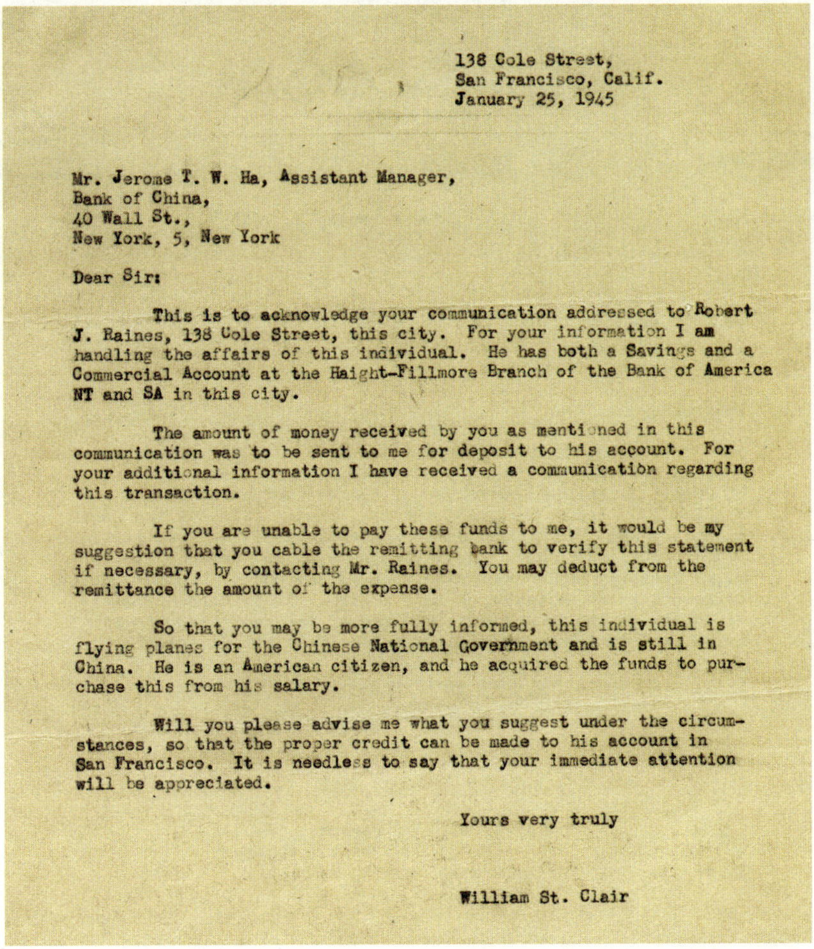

138 Cole Street,
San Francisco, Calif.
January 25, 1945

Mr. Jerome T. W. Ha, Assistant Manager,
Bank of China,
40 Wall St.,
New York, 5, New York

Dear Sir:

This is to acknowledge your communication addressed to Robert J. Raines, 138 Cole Street, this city. For your information I am handling the affairs of this individual. He has both a Savings and a Commercial Account at the Haight-Fillmore Branch of the Bank of America NT and SA in this city.

The amount of money received by you as mentioned in this communication was to be sent to me for deposit to his account. For your additional information I have received a communication regarding this transaction.

If you are unable to pay these funds to me, it would be my suggestion that you cable the remitting bank to verify this statement if necessary, by contacting Mr. Raines. You may deduct from the remittance the amount of the expense.

So that you may be more fully informed, this individual is flying planes for the Chinese National Government and is still in China. He is an American citizen, and he acquired the funds to purchase this from his salary.

Will you please advise me what you suggest under the circumstances, so that the proper credit can be made to his account in San Francisco. It is needless to say that your immediate attention will be appreciated.

Yours very truly

William St. Clair

1945年1月25日，雷恩的家人威廉・圣克莱尔给中国银行银行纽约分行的副经理杰罗姆先生回信。信中再一次明确收件地址是加利福尼亚州旧金山科尔大街138号。信中感谢杰罗姆来信告知，并就雷恩汇款支付等相关事宜提出意见。

A letter from William St. Clair representing Raine receiving the money, February 1st, 1945.

中国银行纽约分行给雷恩亲属的回信

A letter from Bank of China

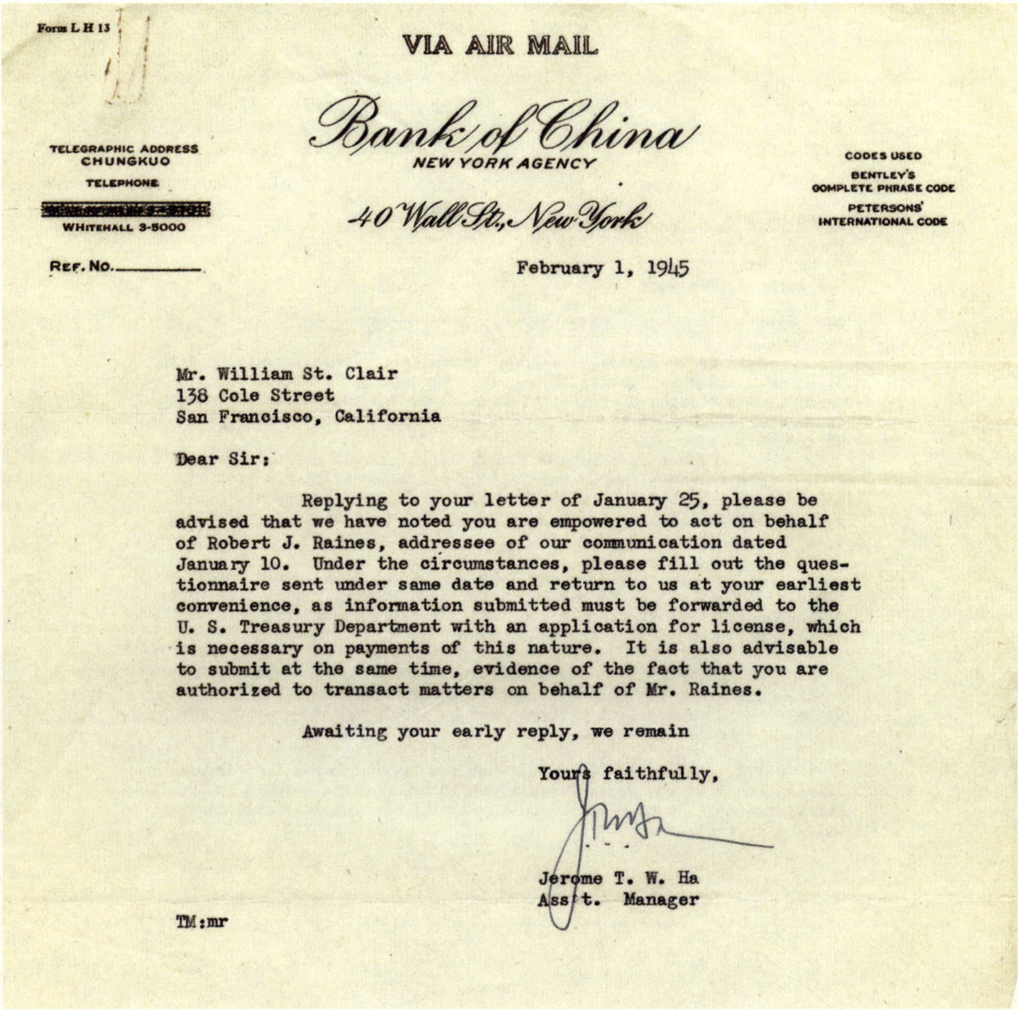

Form L H 13

VIA AIR MAIL

Bank of China

NEW YORK AGENCY

40 Wall St., New York

TELEGRAPHIC ADDRESS
CHUNGKUO

TELEPHONE
[redacted]
WHITEHALL 3-5000

CODES USED
BENTLEY'S
COMPLETE PHRASE CODE
PETERSONS'
INTERNATIONAL CODE

REF. NO.__________

February 1, 1945

Mr. William St. Clair
138 Cole Street
San Francisco, California

Dear Sir:

Replying to your letter of January 25, please be advised that we have noted you are empowered to act on behalf of Robert J. Raines, addressee of our communication dated January 10. Under the circumstances, please fill out the questionnaire sent under same date and return to us at your earliest convenience, as information submitted must be forwarded to the U. S. Treasury Department with an application for license, which is necessary on payments of this nature. It is also advisable to submit at the same time, evidence of the fact that you are authorized to transact matters on behalf of Mr. Raines.

Awaiting your early reply, we remain

Yours faithfully,

Jerome T. W. Ha
Ass't. Manager

TM:mr

1945年2月1日，中国银行纽约分行副经理杰罗姆先生再次给雷恩亲属威廉·圣克莱尔回信，再次请求雷恩亲属尽早填写相关调查表并反馈回中国银行，银行将尽快到财政部办理支付汇款所需的许可证事宜。

A letter from Bank of China, February 1st, 1945.

中国航空公司答复雷恩的函件

CNAC memorandum to Raine

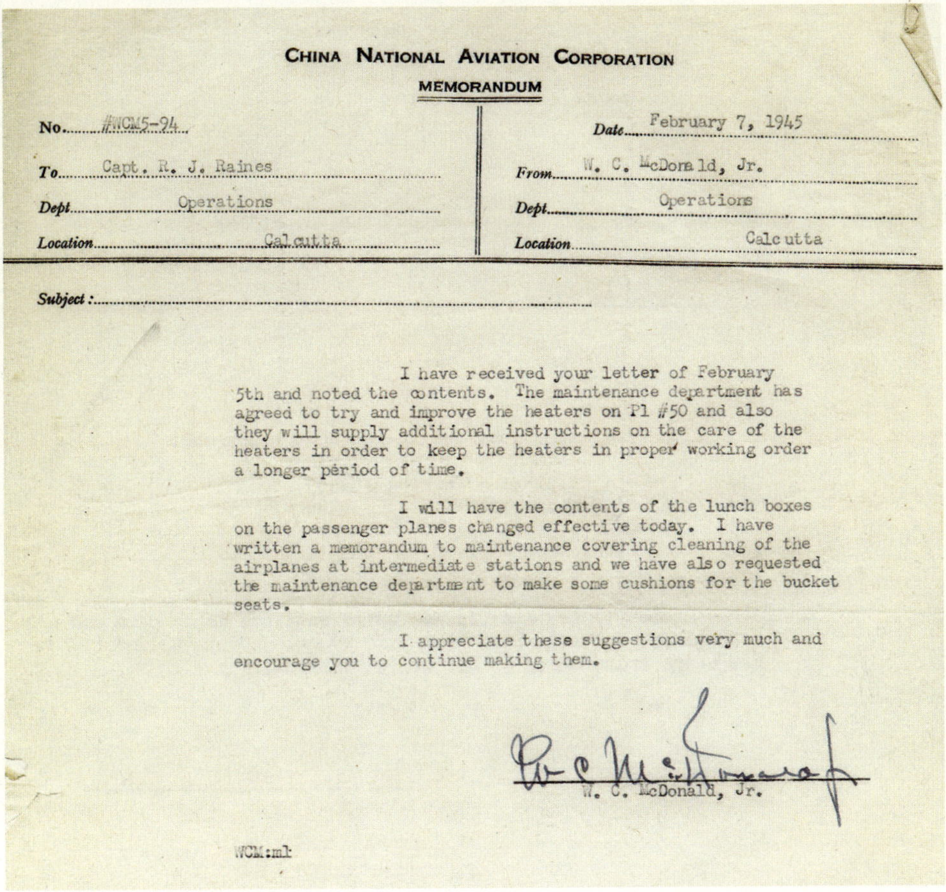

CHINA NATIONAL AVIATION CORPORATION

MEMORANDUM

No. #WCM5-94 | Date February 7, 1945

To Capt. R. J. Raines | From W. C. McDonald, Jr.

Dept Operations | Dept Operations

Location Calcutta | Location Calcutta

Subject :

I have received your letter of February 5th and noted the contents. The maintenance department has agreed to try and improve the heaters on Pl #50 and also they will supply additional instructions on the care of the heaters in order to keep the heaters in proper working order a longer period of time.

I will have the contents of the lunch boxes on the passenger planes changed effective today. I have written a memorandum to maintenance covering cleaning of the airplanes at intermediate stations and we have also requested the maintenance department to make some cushions for the bucket seats.

I appreciate these suggestions very much and encourage you to continue making them.

W. C. McDonald, Jr.

WCM:ml

1945年2月7日，中国航空公司麦克唐纳先生签署的函件，签署地点在加尔各答。麦克唐纳先生答复雷恩：他已于2月5日收悉来信，并就中国航空公司设备维修改良、提高客运服务、飞机养护等工作进行了交流和沟通。其中提及维修部已经同意努力改良热水器设备；改善服务，在客机上提供午餐；在中转站维修保洁飞机；并要求维修部在斗式座椅上加装坐垫等事宜。麦克唐纳先生还衷心感谢雷恩提出诸多的建议性意见。

CNAC memorandum to Raine about his suggestion on aircraft maintenance, February 7th, 1945.

雷恩有关枪械管理的便条副本

A note to Raine regarding Guns

February 15, 1945

Capt. W. C. McDonald, Jr.
Operations
Calcutta

R. J. Raines
Operations
Calcutta

COPY

The following guns are in the CNAC stockroom:

(1) .38 Spl Revolver serial #21569
(2) .22 Hi Standard Pistol 39285
(3) .38 Short Pistol None
(4) 405 Winchester Rifle 65431
(5) 12 gauge Browning Shotgun 60388

Guns (1) (2) and (3) are being retained in my name and renewal fees for same have been paid by me. Guns (4) and (5) are being transferred to Dr. L. J. Richards.

1945年2月15日的便条副本中，明确记录了中国航空公司储物室内存放的5只枪械的具体信息。枪械的名称和枪号都明确记录在案。其中编号1至3号的枪械记录保存在雷恩的名下，编号4至5号的枪械转让给理查德使用。

A note to Raine regarding Guns in CNAC stockroom, February 15th, 1945.

给麦克唐纳的便条

A note to Raine regarding refrigerator

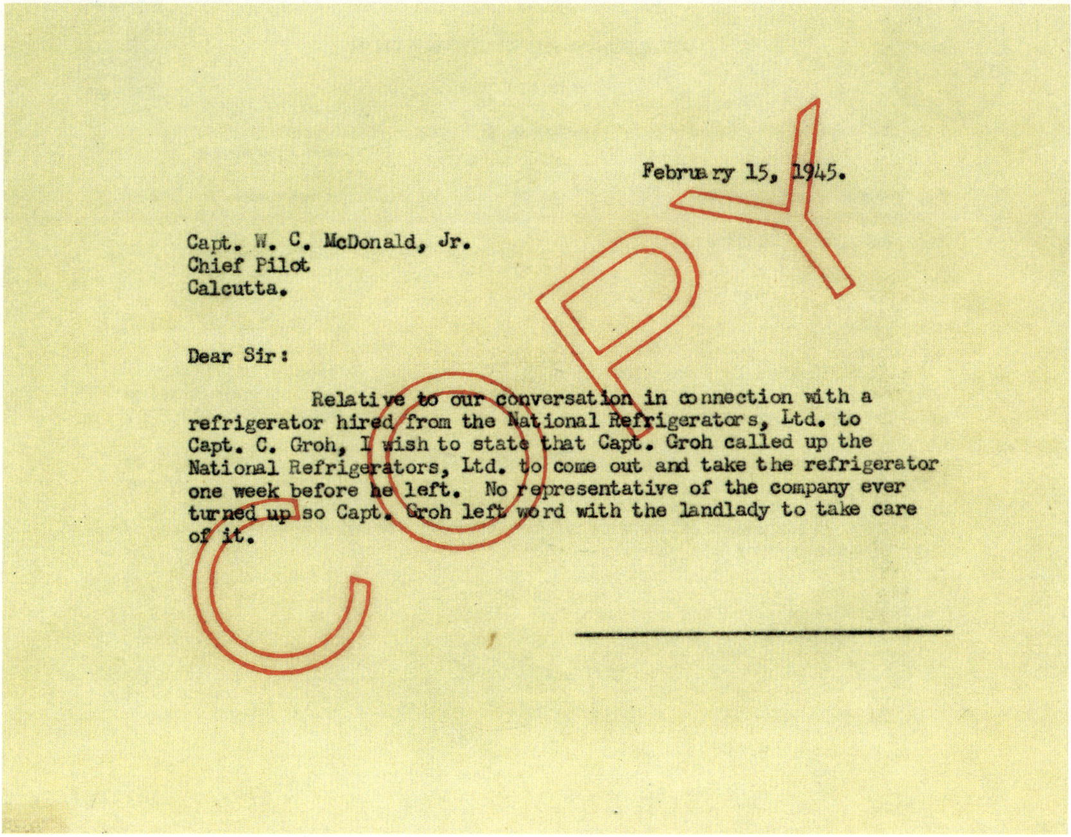

February 15, 1945.

Capt. W. C. McDonald, Jr.
Chief Pilot
Calcutta.

Dear Sir:

Relative to our conversation in connection with a refrigerator hired from the National Refrigerators, Ltd. to Capt. C. Groh, I wish to state that Capt. Groh called up the National Refrigerators, Ltd. to come out and take the refrigerator one week before he left. No representative of the company ever turned up so Capt. Groh left word with the landlady to take care of it.

COPY

1945年2月15日给加尔各答的主飞行员麦克唐纳上尉的便条。拜托麦克唐纳机长转告格罗机长联系办理租用国立冰箱公司冰柜事宜。

A note to someone regarding refrigerator.

退伍军人部回复雷恩的信

A Letter from Veterans Administration

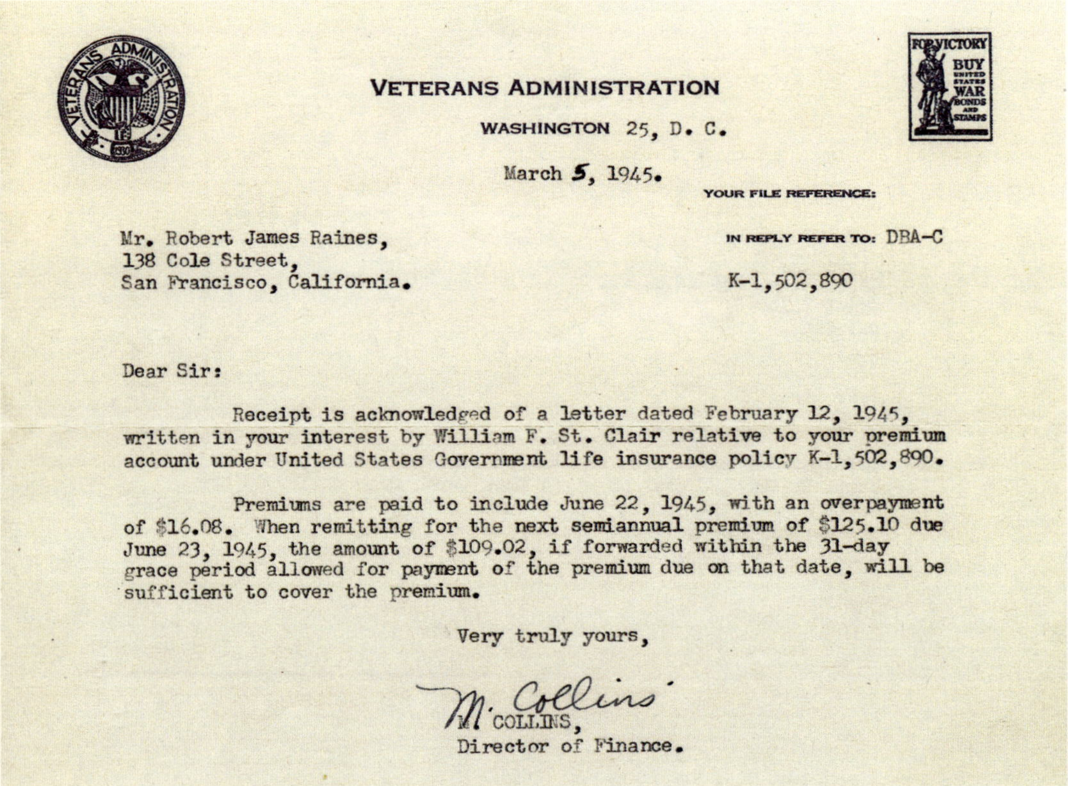

VETERANS ADMINISTRATION

WASHINGTON 25, D. C.

March 5, 1945.

YOUR FILE REFERENCE:

IN REPLY REFER TO: DBA-C

K-1,502,890

Mr. Robert James Raines,
138 Cole Street,
San Francisco, California.

Dear Sir:

Receipt is acknowledged of a letter dated February 12, 1945, written in your interest by William F. St. Clair relative to your premium account under United States Government life insurance policy K-1,502,890.

Premiums are paid to include June 22, 1945, with an overpayment of $16.08. When remitting for the next semiannual premium of $125.10 due June 23, 1945, the amount of $109.02, if forwarded within the 31-day grace period allowed for payment of the premium due on that date, will be sufficient to cover the premium.

Very truly yours,

M. Collins
M. COLLINS,
Director of Finance.

1945年3月5日，退伍军人部回复雷恩有关人寿保险的信件。由财务总监科林斯亲笔签名。雷恩收信地址为加利福尼亚洲日金山科尔大街138号。信中提及雷恩的人寿保险相关事宜授权其亲属威廉.圣克莱尔办理，保险单号为K-1,502,890。信中对保险支付的相关事宜进行了详细的说明和解释：保险费中，扣除1945年6月22日多付的16.08美元，1945年6月23日应缴纳下半年的保险费为125.02美元，实际应缴保费为109.02美元。如果在31天的宽限期内支付保费，将足以支付保费。

A Letter from Veterans Administration to Raine regarding his life insurance, March 5th, 1945.

泛美航空公司证明雷恩为资深飞行员的信件

A letter from American Airways System

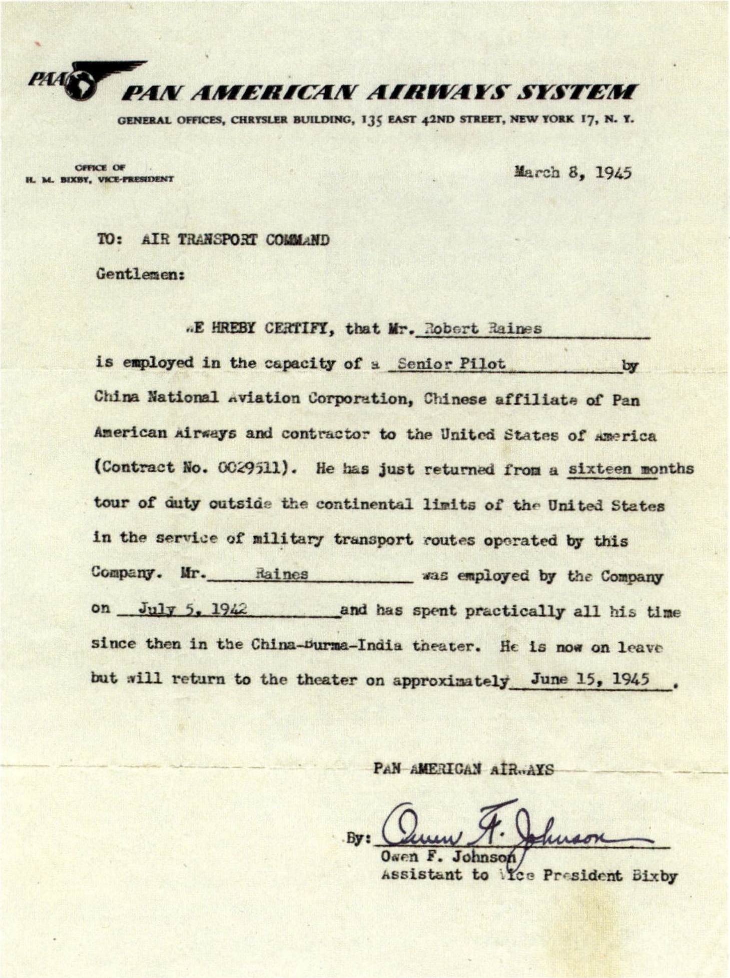

PAA PAN AMERICAN AIRWAYS SYSTEM

GENERAL OFFICES, CHRYSLER BUILDING, 135 EAST 42ND STREET, NEW YORK 17, N. Y.

OFFICE OF
H. M. BIXBY, VICE-PRESIDENT

March 8, 1945

TO: AIR TRANSPORT COMMAND

Gentlemen:

WE HREBY CERTIFY, that Mr. Robert Raines is employed in the capacity of a Senior Pilot by China National Aviation Corporation, Chinese affiliate of Pan American Airways and contractor to the United States of America (Contract No. 0029511). He has just returned from a sixteen months tour of duty outside the continental limits of the United States in the service of military transport routes operated by this Company. Mr. Raines was employed by the Company on July 5, 1942 and has spent practically all his time since then in the China-Burma-India theater. He is now on leave but will return to the theater on approximately June 15, 1945.

PAN AMERICAN AIRWAYS

By: Owen F. Johnson
Owen F. Johnson
Assistant to Vice President Bixby

泛美航空公司1945年3月8日给航空运输司令部的信件，证明雷恩是中国航空公司的资深飞行员。雷恩和美国泛美航空公司签约，编号为0029511。因为泛美航空购买了中国航空公司成立时的美方股份，为中国航空公司注入资金，提供先进的管理经验，是中国航空公司的实际控股人。信中雷恩1942年7月5日受雇于中国航空公司，飞行在中缅印战区的上空。此时他离开返回美国，将在1945年6月15日重返战区。

Background: Pan American World Airways bought American shares in the CNAC at its inception, and injected capital into the CNAC and provided technical know-how. Pan-Am was the actual holding company of CNAC.

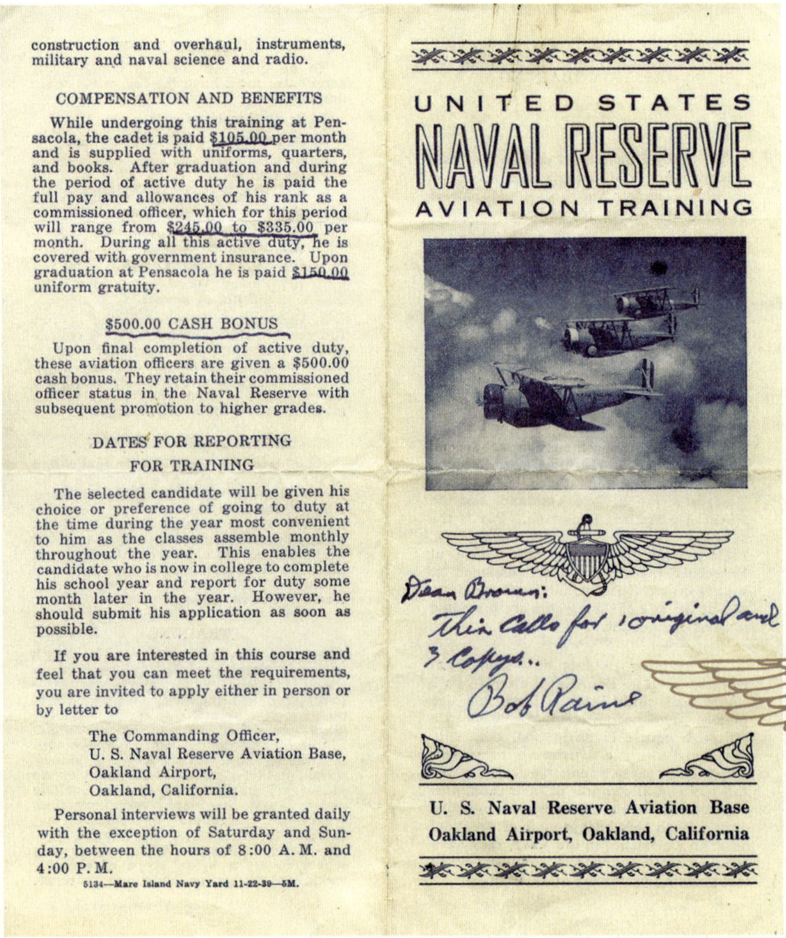

construction and overhaul, instruments, military and naval science and radio.

COMPENSATION AND BENEFITS

While undergoing this training at Pensacola, the cadet is paid $105.00 per month and is supplied with uniforms, quarters, and books. After graduation and during the period of active duty he is paid the full pay and allowances of his rank as a commissioned officer, which for this period will range from $245.00 to $335.00 per month. During all this active duty, he is covered with government insurance. Upon graduation at Pensacola he is paid $150.00 uniform gratuity.

$500.00 CASH BONUS

Upon final completion of active duty, these aviation officers are given a $500.00 cash bonus. They retain their commissioned officer status in the Naval Reserve with subsequent promotion to higher grades.

DATES FOR REPORTING FOR TRAINING

The selected candidate will be given his choice or preference of going to duty at the time during the year most convenient to him as the classes assemble monthly throughout the year. This enables the candidate who is now in college to complete his school year and report for duty some month later in the year. However, he should submit his application as soon as possible.

If you are interested in this course and feel that you can meet the requirements, you are invited to apply either in person or by letter to

The Commanding Officer,
U. S. Naval Reserve Aviation Base,
Oakland Airport,
Oakland, California.

Personal interviews will be granted daily with the exception of Saturday and Sunday, between the hours of 8:00 A. M. and 4:00 P. M.

5134—Mare Island Navy Yard 11-22-39—5M.

UNITED STATES
NAVAL RESERVE
AVIATION TRAINING

Dear Brown:
This calls for 1 original and 3 copys..
Bob Raine

U. S. Naval Reserve Aviation Base
Oakland Airport, Oakland, California

介绍美国海军后备队航空训练步骤、阶段、申请人须具备的条件和资格、选拔方式、培训课程、补贴津贴福利、公布时间及联系方式。在资料后空白处有雷恩写给布朗的一句话，“这份原始资料复制3份”。

An introduction of the procedures, phases, qualifications for applicants, tests, curricula, compensation and benefits, date of issue and mailing address.

雷恩的银行存款收条

Bank of America's Savings Deposited for Account

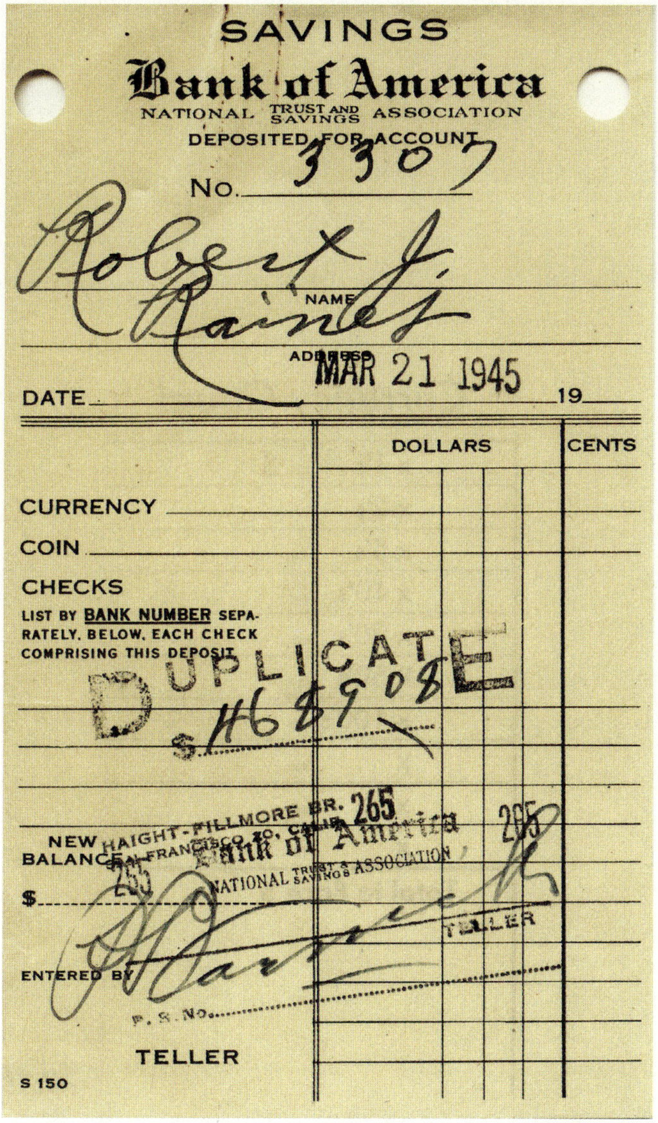

SAVINGS
Bank of America
NATIONAL TRUST AND SAVINGS ASSOCIATION
DEPOSITED FOR ACCOUNT
No. 3307
Robert J. Raine
NAME
ADDRESS MAR 21 1945
DATE 19
DOLLARS CENTS
CURRENCY
COIN
CHECKS
LIST BY BANK NUMBER SEPARATELY, BELOW, EACH CHECK COMPRISING THIS DEPOSIT
DUPLICATE
$ 1168908
HAIGHT-FILLMORE BR. 265
SAN FRANCISCO, CALIF.
Bank of America
NATIONAL TRUST & SAVINGS ASSOCIATION
265
NEW BALANCE 265
$
TELLER
ENTERED BY
P. S. No.
TELLER
S 150

1945年3月21日回到美国的雷恩在美国银行的存款单据。

Bank of America's Savings Deposited for Account #3307, R. J. Raine, March 21st, 1945.

这是1945年6月10日，志愿队财务主管帕克斯顿亲笔签名给志愿队成员的信。信中公开了志愿队的费用支出明细、志愿队年鉴、书籍、纪念基金等内容。

志愿队的费用支出明细如下：

100 架P-40战斗机购置费：750万美元;

战机购置佣金：25万美元;

运费，保险费等：254,267.46美元

中央飞机制造公司筹划费：2,995,732.54美元

共计1100万美元

其中中央飞机制造公司筹划费具体包括以下明细：

现金及应收款：323,985.58美元

工资：1,551,187.55美元

死亡抚恤金：83,100.00美元

胜利奖金：148,499.87美元

旅行及搬运费：577,472.19美元

分站，邮费，电报，家具：40,674.54美元

租金：13,639.32美元

空运费：28,076.91美元

管理飞机费：104,298.09美元

住宿及劳工费：33,468.26美元

工具、修理及配件：29,523.45美元

马尼拉希科克公司费用：25,000.00美元

杂费等 ：36,806.78美元

合计2,995,732.54美元

To "Veteran of the AVG" document from G.L. Paxton summarizing the expenses incurred by the AVG, yearbook, books, memorial fund and many other items, June 10th, 1945.

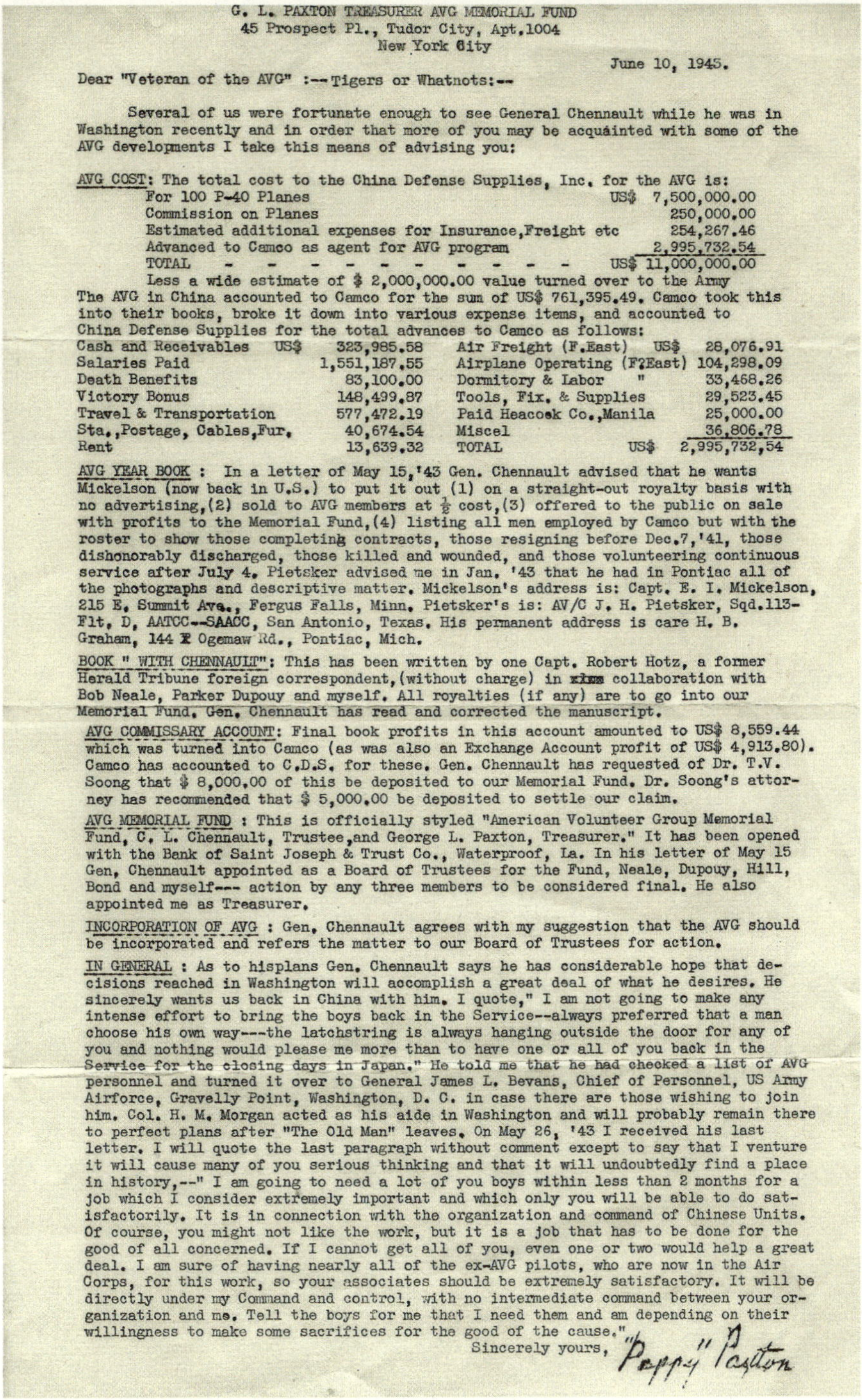

G. L. PAXTON TREASURER AVG MEMORIAL FUND
45 Prospect Pl., Tudor City, Apt.1004
New York City

June 10, 1945.

Dear "Veteran of the AVG" :--Tigers or Whatnots:--

Several of us were fortunate enough to see General Chennault while he was in Washington recently and in order that more of you may be acquainted with some of the AVG developments I take this means of advising you:

AVG COST: The total cost to the China Defense Supplies, Inc. for the AVG is:

For 100 P-40 Planes	US$ 7,500,000.00
Commission on Planes	250,000.00
Estimated additional expenses for Insurance,Freight etc	254,267.46
Advanced to Camco as agent for AVG program	2,995,732.54
TOTAL - - - - - - - - - - - - -	US$ 11,000,000.00

Less a wide estimate of $ 2,000,000.00 value turned over to the Army
The AVG in China accounted to Camco for the sum of US$ 761,395.49. Camco took this into their books, broke it down into various expense items, and accounted to China Defense Supplies for the total advances to Camco as follows:

Cash and Receivables	US$ 323,985.58	Air Freight (F.East)	US$ 28,076.91
Salaries Paid	1,551,187.55	Airplane Operating (F?East)	104,298.09
Death Benefits	83,100.00	Dormitory & Labor "	33,468.26
Victory Bonus	148,499.87	Tools, Fix. & Supplies	29,523.45
Travel & Transportation	577,472.19	Paid Heacock Co.,Manila	25,000.00
Sta.,Postage, Cables,Fur.	40,674.54	Miscel	36,806.78
Rent	13,639.32	TOTAL	US$ 2,995,732,54

AVG YEAR BOOK : In a letter of May 15,'43 Gen. Chennault advised that he wants Mickelson (now back in U.S.) to put it out (1) on a straight-out royalty basis with no advertising,(2) sold to AVG members at ½ cost,(3) offered to the public on sale with profits to the Memorial Fund,(4) listing all men employed by Camco but with the roster to show those completing contracts, those resigning before Dec.7,'41, those dishonorably discharged, those killed and wounded, and those volunteering continuous service after July 4. Pietsker advised me in Jan. '43 that he had in Pontiac all of the photographs and descriptive matter. Mickelson's address is: Capt. E. I. Mickelson, 215 E. Summit Ave., Fergus Falls, Minn. Pietsker's is: AV/C J. H. Pietsker, Sqd.113-Flt. D, AATCC--SAACC, San Antonio, Texas. His permanent address is care H. B. Graham, 144 E Ogemaw Rd., Pontiac, Mich.

BOOK " WITH CHENNAULT": This has been written by one Capt. Robert Hotz, a former Herald Tribune foreign correspondent,(without charge) in ~~xixx~~ collaboration with Bob Neale, Parker Dupouy and myself. All royalties (if any) are to go into our Memorial Fund. Gen. Chennault has read and corrected the manuscript.

AVG COMMISSARY ACCOUNT: Final book profits in this account amounted to US$ 8,559.44 which was turned into Camco (as was also an Exchange Account profit of US$ 4,913.80). Camco has accounted to C.D.S. for these. Gen. Chennault has requested of Dr. T.V. Soong that $ 8,000.00 of this be deposited to our Memorial Fund. Dr. Soong's attorney has recommended that $ 5,000.00 be deposited to settle our claim.

AVG MEMORIAL FUND : This is officially styled "American Volunteer Group Memorial Fund, C. L. Chennault, Trustee,and George L. Paxton, Treasurer." It has been opened with the Bank of Saint Joseph & Trust Co., Waterproof, La. In his letter of May 15 Gen. Chennault appointed as a Board of Trustees for the Fund, Neale, Dupouy, Hill, Bond and myself--- action by any three members to be considered final. He also appointed me as Treasurer.

INCORPORATION OF AVG : Gen. Chennault agrees with my suggestion that the AVG should be incorporated and refers the matter to our Board of Trustees for action.

IN GENERAL : As to hisplans Gen. Chennault says he has considerable hope that decisions reached in Washington will accomplish a great deal of what he desires. He sincerely wants us back in China with him. I quote," I am not going to make any intense effort to bring the boys back in the Service--always preferred that a man choose his own way---the latchstring is always hanging outside the door for any of you and nothing would please me more than to have one or all of you back in the Service for the closing days in Japan." He told me that he had checked a list of AVG personnel and turned it over to General James L. Bevans, Chief of Personnel, US Army Airforce, Gravelly Point, Washington, D. C. in case there are those wishing to join him. Col. H. M. Morgan acted as his aide in Washington and will probably remain there to perfect plans after "The Old Man" leaves. On May 26, '43 I received his last letter. I will quote the last paragraph without comment except to say that I venture it will cause many of you serious thinking and that it will undoubtedly find a place in history,--" I am going to need a lot of you boys within less than 2 months for a job which I consider extremely important and which only you will be able to do satisfactorily. It is in connection with the organization and command of Chinese Units. Of course, you might not like the work, but it is a job that has to be done for the good of all concerned. If I cannot get all of you, even one or two would help a great deal. I am sure of having nearly all of the ex-AVG pilots, who are now in the Air Corps, for this work, so your associates should be extremely satisfactory. It will be directly under my Command and control, with no intermediate command between your organization and me. Tell the boys for me that I need them and am depending on their willingness to make some sacrifices for the good of the cause."

Sincerely yours, "Poppy" Paxton

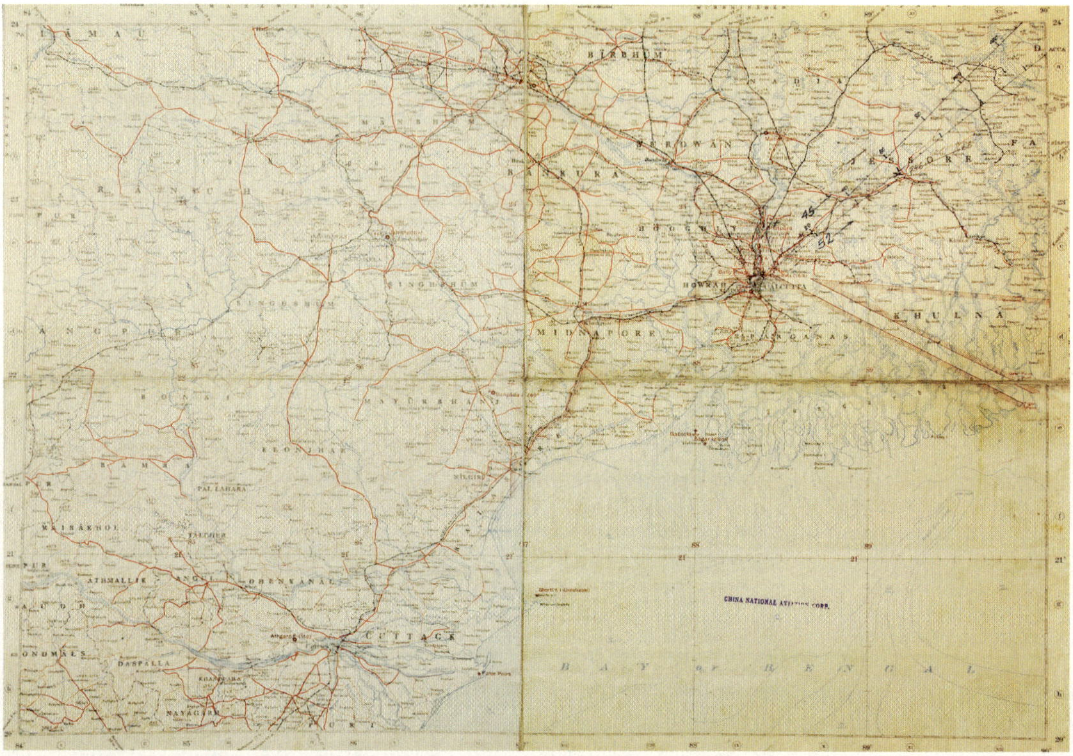

地图于1940年印刷，纸质，印度地图。地图面积较大，折叠为四层，方便携带。雷恩就职于中国航空公司期间，印度是其主要的飞行活动区域。在雷恩的很多纸质文件中，有许多在印度东北部城市加尔各答签署，也证实了雷恩往来于印度的史实。

【背景知识】：中国航空公司是中华民国政府与美国柯蒂斯–赖特飞机公司合资成立的航空公司。1942年下半年后，在陈纳德指挥下，中国航空公司发展迅速。印度阿萨姆的汀江和中国云南昆明成为主要航行基地。在飞机行员方面，因美国援华志愿航空队解散中国航空公司获得了10余名AVG飞行员，雷恩即为其中成员之一。中国抗日战争期间，中国航空公司作为驼峰空运的主要力量，往返于印中两国运送物资和人员，为中国抗战作出了重要贡献。

It is four-folded. During his service in CNAC, Raine's major air route was to India.

Background: CNAC was established as a joint venture between KMT government and the U.S. Pan-American World Airways. From the latter half of 1942, under the leadership of Claire Lee Chennault, CNAC developed by leap and bounds. Dinjan in Assam, India and Kunming in Yunnan province, China became the major airfields for CNAC. After the dissolution of AVG, CNAC recruited a dozen volunteer pilots and Raine was one of them.

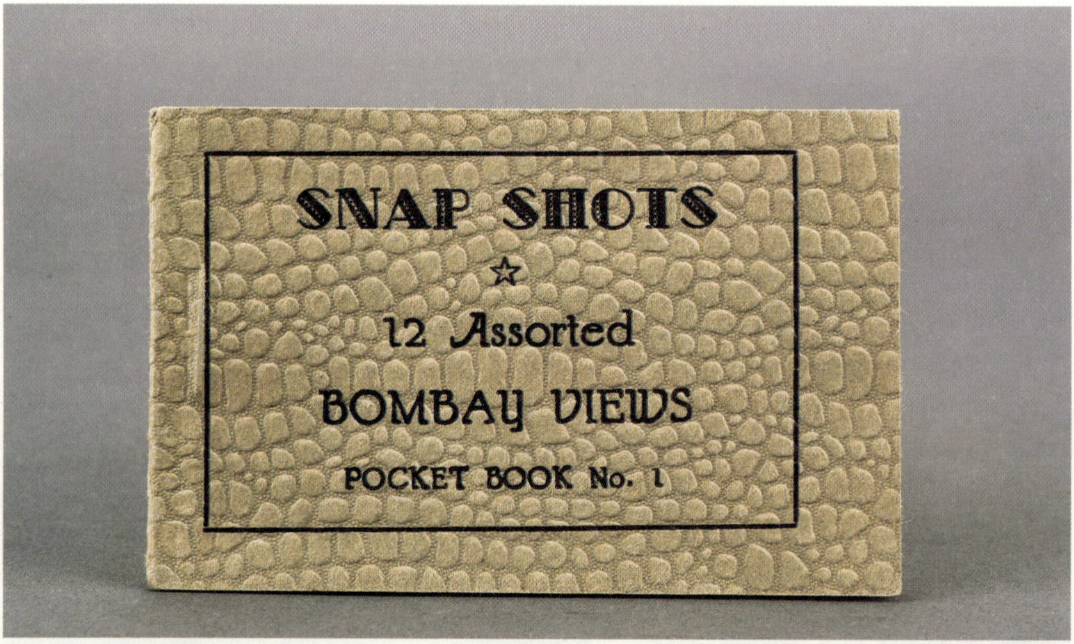

1945年出版的纸质图册，内容是印度孟买12景，均为孟买当时标志性古典建筑和历史遗迹。

The photo brochure, published in 1945, was about the 12 tourist attractions in Bombay, which included the historic landmarks of the city.

中国航空公司和各地酒店标志
Logos of CNAC and some hotels

均为纸质彩色椭圆形或圆形标志，颜色不一。其中中国航空公司标志4张，酒店标志3张。中国航空公司标志为圆形或椭圆形，上有中文或者英文标志，有的配有飞机或者飞翼的图案装饰；酒店标志为印度加尔各答大酒店、卡拉奇基拉尼酒店标志。

Paper texture, circular and oval colored logos, 4 logos of CNAC and 3 logos of hotels.

雷恩保留的各国钱币

Chinese, Burmese, Indian and other paper currencies collected by Raine

雷恩经历丰富，曾辗转于中国、缅甸、印度等多个国家，因此保留了许多国家的钱币。在雷恩保留的各国钱币中，除了有大量的中华民国纸币外，还有印度、缅甸、埃及等国的钱币。

Raine traveled to many parts of the world including China, Burma and India, so he had a collection of coins and paper currency of the countries he had been to.

中央航空公司徽章
Badge of CATC

金色飞翼徽章，正面中心饰圆形白地蓝纹图案，上书"CATC"大写的英文字母，为Central Air Transport Corporation的缩写，即中央航空运输有限公司。中央航空运输有限公司是由国民政府交通部与航委会于1943年3月1日正式成立，隶属交通部的国营民航企业。中央航运公司刚成立时，总公司暂设在昆明，由当时交通部航政司司长何墨林任该公司董事长，委派空军上校陈卓林出任总经理。中央航运公司雇佣有许多外籍飞行员。

Golden Spread Wings Badge, with a white and blue disc at the center, CATC short for Central Air Transport Corporation. CATC, a state-run enterprise, was established on March 1st, 1943 by the Ministry of Transportation and Commission of Aviation under the KMT government. At its inception, CATC was based in Kunming and led by Mr. He Molin, then director of Aviation Administration of the Ministry of Transportation as the chairman of the board, and Colonel Chen Zhuolin from the air force as the general manager. CATC recruited a team of foreign pilots.

中央航空公司飞行员头箍金银徽章

CATC cap badge with hat band.

黑布地，中心饰金丝徽章图案，并书“CATC”大写的英文字母，是中央航空运输有限公司的英文缩写。

Black cloth texture, gold wire pattern at the center, CATC short for Central Air Transport Corporation.

飞虎队员普雷斯科特给雷恩的信

Letter from AVG member R. W. Prescott to Raine

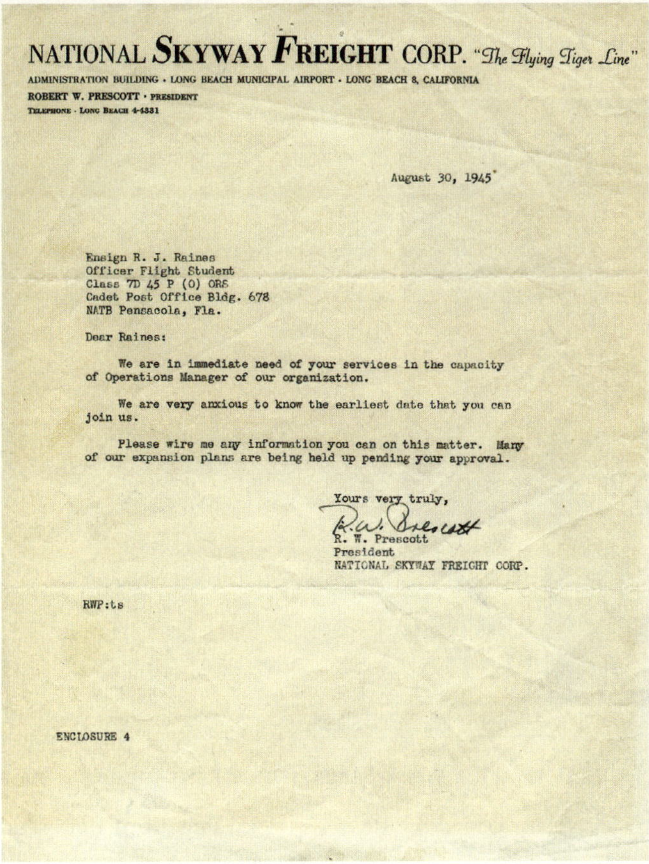

NATIONAL SKYWAY FREIGHT CORP. "The Flying Tiger Line"
ADMINISTRATION BUILDING · LONG BEACH MUNICIPAL AIRPORT · LONG BEACH 8, CALIFORNIA
ROBERT W. PRESCOTT · PRESIDENT
TELEPHONE · LONG BEACH 4-4331

August 30, 1945

Ensign R. J. Raines
Officer Flight Student
Class 7D 45 P (O) OR5
Cadet Post Office Bldg. 678
NATB Pensacola, Fla.

Dear Raines:

We are in immediate need of your services in the capacity of Operations Manager of our organization.

We are very anxious to know the earliest date that you can join us.

Please wire me any information you can on this matter. Many of our expansion plans are being held up pending your approval.

Yours very truly,
R.W. Prescott
R. W. Prescott
President
NATIONAL SKYWAY FREIGHT CORP.

RWP:ts

ENCLOSURE 4

全国天空货运公司董事长罗伯特·普雷斯科特1945年8月30日邀请雷恩加入的亲笔签名信。罗伯特·普雷斯科特为原志愿队第2中队成员。1945年6月罗伯特·普雷斯科特创办全国天空货运公司，后改名为飞虎航空公司。之后飞虎航空公司发展成为当时全球第一家定期的货运航空公司。此时雷恩为海军少尉，在佛罗里达州的彭萨科拉海军军官培训基地接受培训。最终雷恩与另外12位飞行员以原始股东身份加入了罗伯特·普雷斯科特为董事长的飞虎航空公司。

R. W. Prescott, President of National Skyway Freight Corp (NSFC) wrote a letter to Raine on August 30th, 1945 to invite him to join his company. Prescott, a former member of the 2nd squadron of AVG, established the National Skyway Freight Corp in June 1945, later the named changed into Flying Tiger Line. Flying Tiger Line developed into the first regular air freight company in the world. By the time of the establishment of the company, Raine, an ensign in US navy, was taking training in the Pensacola Navy Flight School in Florida. Raine and other 12 pilots joined Prescott's Flying Tiger Line as shareholders.

洛杉矶时报主办的《本周》杂志，1945年11月4日在第4页有全国天空货运公司相关的报道。此时由12个飞虎队员组成的全国天空货运公司刚组建不久，还未更名为飞虎航运公司。公司核心领导均为飞虎队员，如董事长罗伯特·普雷斯科特、首席飞行员约瑟夫·罗伯特、机械师迈克·韦克菲尔德、飞机工程师哈维等。

This Week Magazine of Los Angeles Times issued on Nov. 4th, 1945. Page 4 of this issue carried a report on National Skyway Freight Corp, which was established just before its name was changed into Flying Tiger Line. The top management of this corporation were former members of the Flying Tigers, including the president Prescott, chief pilot Joseph Rosbert, mechanic Mike Wakefield, aircraft engineer Harvey, etc.

FLYING TIGERS FLY AGAIN

by Adie Suehsdorf

These men made history in China. Now they've power-dived into the air freight market. A real postwar success story

WARM UP: Stocky Jack Cornelius left an airline job to take over the engineering of the Conestogas

THE stocky Conestoga cargo plane pounded down the runway at Salinas and was airborne. It climbed slowly and easily, with the morning sun flashing along its stainless steel body. Aboard, bound for Atlanta, were five tons of strawberries freshly picked from the long green valley flattening out below.

At 10,000 feet — shoulder high to the Sierras — the pilot leveled off, set his course and relaxed. The Conestoga bored eastward. On the tail, in new red paint, were the words, "The Flying Tiger Line." The Flying Tigers were flying again.

Moreover, as subsequent flights have shown, they are flying with the old flair, with all the old audacity. **For 12 of the Tigers, averaging in age slightly more than a ripe 29 years, have formed an airline and power-dived into the great and unexplored post-war market for air freight.**

Their new outfit is the National Skyway [illegible]ation, the first transcontinental, all-cargo airline in the United States. They are based at Long Beach, Calif., with a small fleet of Conestogas, and offer 24-hour, coast-to-coast air freight service.

Help Hog-Tie Oil Well

ALTHOUGH flying for only three months, the Flying Tiger Line has already rushed 275 pounds of emergency machinery from New York to Fort Worth to hog-tie a rampaging oil well, flown Bakersfield grapes and cantaloupes to Detroit, made many other trips.

Hollywood wants the Tigers to fly studio sets and props to movie companies on location. And California horsemen have been crying for space in which to ship their racers.

Hauling freight is not fighting Jap Zeroes, and the Conestogas are not P-40's, but there has been no change in the men. They are still Flying Tigers. This must be kept in mind if you are to understand how their airline was formed and how it operates.

A few years back, they were the American Volunteer Group, General Claire Chennault's inspired free-lances, who ranged Asia's skies, singlehandedly taking on the Japanese air force. Between 1941 and 1942, they officially knocked out 297 Japanese planes.

They shot Zeroes off each others' tails. They relieved their tension under the glow of Bob Prescott's easy good-fellowship. They drew strength from cool "Duke" Hedman, who once made five kills in one day. Again and again, their lives depended on crew chiefs like Jack Cornelius, whose skillful improvisations kept the battered P-40's aloft.

It sounds melodramatic to say these things now, but they have a bearing. For the Tigers' roots are in the past and experience and memory weld them together today.

Their airline started several months ago when Bob Prescott stumbled across 14 surplus Conestogas begging to be bought. A keen-eyed Texan of 32, he knew a good airplane when he saw one. He liked the deep-chested, thin-flanked Conestoga. It was designed for cargo; not a flashy performer, but economical and steady. And the price was right. The Reconstruction Finance Corporation was letting them go for a little over $400,000.

They'd Fly Anywhere, Any Time

THE Flying Tiger Line began to take shape in Prescott's mind. It would be a contract airline; fly anywhere, any time, but only on demand. It would need no franchise, would be bound to no rigid schedules requiring flights whether or not there was a payload aboard. Furthermore, if the Tigers would run it with him, they could fly the planes themselves and cut operating costs to the bone. The more he thought about it, the better he liked it.

He telephoned "Duke" Hedman in New York and "Catfish" Raines in Los Angeles. "Let's get the guys together and see what we can make of it."

No one had to have his arm twisted. Stocky Jack Cornelius, then working as senior engineer for an airline in New York, was the only problem. He resisted for approximately nine seconds. He had been thinking of throwing up aviation to sell electrical appliances in Jackson Heights. That wasn't a proper job for an ex-Tiger, though. And the "Duke's" soft talk persuaded him that the good people of that community should look to someone else for their toasters and waffle irons.

Once converted, Cornelius called Joe Rosbert, of Seattle, who once crashed into a Himalayan peak at 16,000 feet while flying the Hump and lived to tell about it. Joe wanted in, too. He'd recovered and was ready to go.

Mike Wakefield, the Tennessee botanist and orchid specialist who turned AVG mechanic, came in. Carl Brown was studying medicine in Los Angeles, but would pilot short runs at night or over week-ends. Bob King, of Palestine, Tex., whose beacons and air warning nets saved many AVG lives in China, was on tap for radio maintenance.

Then the word spread farther afield. "Bart" Bartling hollered in from Middletown, Ind., and Harvey Wirta spoke up from Chicago. The grapevine even carried to China. There, Dick Rossi, still piloting the Hump for China National Aviation Corporation, and Major "Link" Laughlin, then with the Marines, simply wired $10,000 each to the

4

TW—11-4-45

...dumped
...them, lined
...questions. Not
...where — they just

...starting, would only be stealing from ourselves."

Hitch-Hikers

NATIONAL SKYWAY FREIGHT's first official flight was made late in July. It was about as formal as a barn dance. Prescott, Hedman and Cornelius had gone east to pick up the first of their Conestogas. As they prepared to leave New York's La Guardia Field, several businessmen, bumped off other flights, asked for a ride.

"It'll be no picnic," the Tigers warned. "There's no insulation in this plane, no heat, no stewardesses. If that suits you, hop aboard." They all hopped.

At Washington there was a three-hour layover while the Tigers conducted some business. When they returned, the New Yorkers had drummed up eight more passengers. At Nashville, four more turned up.

By now it was an outing. At each stop,

...and be an executive.

His wife, Helen Ruth, a former newspaper reporter, has pitched in to help as his secretary. Dorothy Cornelius and Marianne Rosbert are working for their husbands in California.

The Tigers say they'd be set for office help if they could only marry off "Duke" Hedman to a nice girl accountant.

Nevertheless, for a line that was just a gleam in its president's eye on June 1, the National Skyway Freight Corporation has come far. It has plenty of imagination and no fear — which is what you'd expect, after all, from Flying Tigers.

Jack Cornelius summed it up when he said: "We all had good jobs in aviation and we gave them up. We took this one on for life. We're small now, but we're first in a new field and we hope to keep the lead. Why should we worry about anyone else? Let them worry about us."

The End

NOVELTY: A curious crowd gathers whenever one of these planes appears

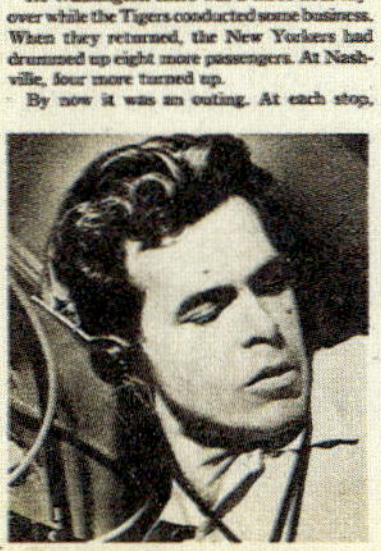

MECHANIC, Mike Wakefield

CHIEF pilot, Joseph Rosbert

BOSS, Robert W. Prescott

FLIGHT engineer, Harvey Wirta

全国天空货运公司徽章

National Skyway Freight Corporation (NSFC) pilot wing

黑色布地，用金银丝线盘绣飞翼展翅造型。飞翼中心有形似地球的球形装饰，球体蓝色，上书“NSFC”大写的英文字母，是全国天空货运公司的英文缩写，后改名为美国飞虎航空公司。

Texture: black cloth, NSFC pilot wing with bullion wings and a round disc with NSFC (short for National Skyway Freight Corp, becoming the Flying Tigers Line later) and blue globe.

飞虎航空公司飞行徽章
Flying Tiger sterling wing

金属质地，精致小巧，形似飞翼展翅，中间为圆形装饰。

Texture: metal, elaborate, spread wings, disc in the middle.

美国飞虎航空公司宣传资料

A brochure of the Flying Tiger Line

1946年美国飞虎航空公司印制的宣传册子，宣传册子中回顾了组成飞虎航空公司的几位飞虎队员的壮举，其中提到了罗伯特·普雷斯科特、“鲶鱼”雷恩、“公爵”赫德曼等。1945年他们在罗伯特·普雷斯科特的设想下组建了全国天空货运公司，后改名为飞虎航空公司。经过一年的发展，飞虎航空公司员工超过250人，在全国各地都设有办事处，公司还添置了几架运输机，娴熟的飞行员、细致的服务、高效的管理，能满足客户的各种运输要求。

A brochure published in 1946 by the Flying Tiger Line, which carried a review of the pilots' exploits in the WWII by mentioning the names of R. W. Prescott, "Catfish" Raine, Robert "Duke" Hedman, etc. Prescott initiated National Skyway Freight Corp in 1945, later the name changed into the Flying Tiger Line.

雷恩行总空运大队服务证

Raine' Identification Card issued by the CNRRA Air Transport

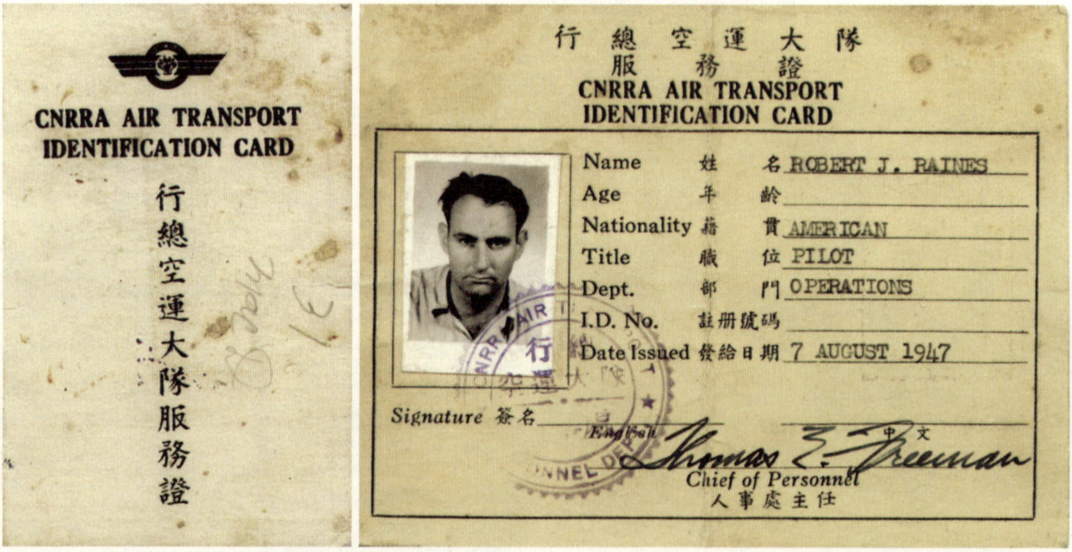

1946年10月，行总空运大队在上海成立，英文名称为CNRRA Air Transport，缩写为CAT。“行总”是“行政院善后救济总署”的简称。董事会由中美双方人员组成。董事会聘请陈纳德为总经理。1947年1月31日，第一架绘有飞虎标徽的C—47型运输机，装载着“行总”救济物资从上海虹桥机场起飞，行总空运队营运正式开始，负责将行政院善后救济物资运输到各地。1948年5月28日，行总空运队改组为民航局直辖空运队。在行总空运大队飞行人员中，有美国志愿队或14航空队队员，雷恩就是其中之一，其服务证签发日期为1947年8月7日。

China National Relief and Rehabilitation Administration (CNRRA) was established in Shanghai in October, 1946. The board of directors of this institution comprised both Chinese and Americans, and Claire Lee Chennault was hired as the general manager. CNRRA Air Transport was responsible for flying relief supplies issued by the Executive Yuan to the disaster-hit areas in China. On May 28th, 1945, CNRRA Air Transport was restructured into the Air Transport Squadron directly under the Civil Aviation Administration. The pilots of the CNRRA Air Transport included former members of AVG and the Fourteenth Air Force, and Raine was one of them. The date of issue of this card is August 7th, 1947.

雷恩在中国的自卫枪支执照

Chinese gun license with his photo for a Smith & Wesson

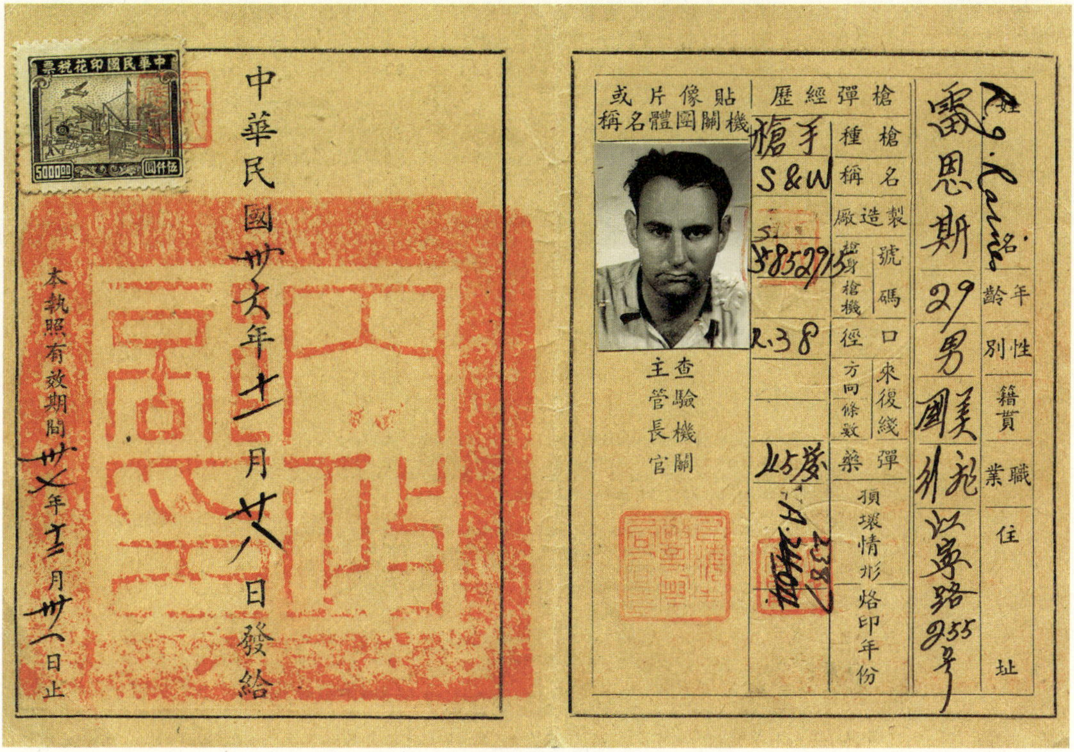

内政部发给雷恩的自卫枪支执照，颁发日期为中华民国36（1947）年11月28日，有效期截止到中华民国37（1948）年12月31日。执照上列有“枪支持用人应注意事项”，雷恩个人信息等，执照上显示雷恩居住在江宁路255号，枪支为手枪，口径为.38。此时的雷恩服务于陈纳德担任总经理的行总空运大队，居住在上海。

By the time of the issue of the gun license, Raine was serving in the CNRRA Air Transport led by Gen. Chennault and living in Shanghai.

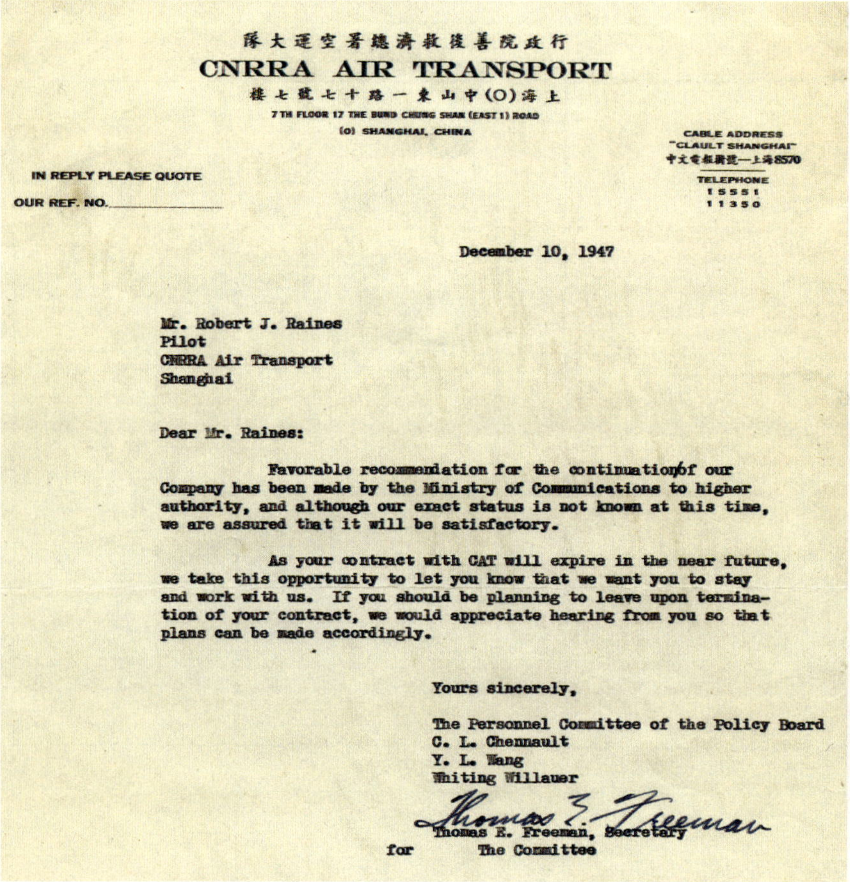

行政院善後救濟總署空運大隊
CNRRA AIR TRANSPORT
上海(O)中山東一路十七號七樓
7TH FLOOR 17 THE BUND CHUNG SHAN (EAST 1) ROAD
(O) SHANGHAI, CHINA

CABLE ADDRESS
"CLAULT SHANGHAI"
中文電報掛號—上海8570
TELEPHONE
15551
11350

IN REPLY PLEASE QUOTE
OUR REF. NO.

December 10, 1947

Mr. Robert J. Raines
Pilot
CNRRA Air Transport
Shanghai

Dear Mr. Raines:

Favorable recommendation for the continuation of our Company has been made by the Ministry of Communications to higher authority, and although our exact status is not known at this time, we are assured that it will be satisfactory.

As your contract with CAT will expire in the near future, we take this opportunity to let you know that we want you to stay and work with us. If you should be planning to leave upon termination of your contract, we would appreciate hearing from you so that plans can be made accordingly.

Yours sincerely,

The Personnel Committee of the Policy Board
C. L. Chennault
Y. L. Wang
Whiting Willauer

Thomas E. Freeman
Thomas E. Freeman, Secretary
for The Committee

行总空运大队于1947年12月10日发出给雷恩的信，信中表示希望雷恩能与行总空运大队再续合约。人事政策委员会陈纳德、怀丁·魏劳尔、王源凌、秘书长托马斯·E.弗里曼签发。此时的行总空运大队正面临着被改组为民航局直辖空运队，其中陈纳德、怀丁·魏劳尔为行总空运大队原董事会成员，王源凌则是改组后民航局直辖空运队的董事长。

The letter dated December 10th, 1947 from CNRRA Air Transport to Raine was about its intention of extending contract with Raine. By the time of the letter, CNRRA Air Transport was about to be restructured into the Air Transport Squadron directly under the Civil Aviation Administration, in which Chennault, Whiting Willauer as members of the board of directors, and Wang Yuanling as the chairman of the board.

雷恩保留的游船菜单

5 menus collected by Raine

雷恩保留的美国海军后备队在克利夫兰总统号游船上的晚餐菜单，共五张，用餐时间是1949年11月，日期分别为12、13、14、17、22日。菜单封面图案各异，色彩绚丽。晚餐菜品众多，分为开胃菜、蔬菜、汤类、沙拉、凉菜、主菜、鱼类、奶酪、甜点等众多种类。克利夫兰总统号是20世纪50年代美国总统轮船公司的一艘来往于中国和美国之间的邮轮的名字，以美国总统格罗弗·克利夫兰名字命名。

5 menus collected by Raine when US navy reserve had dinner on President Cleveland liner. The dates are Nov. 12th, 13th, 14th, 17th, 22nd, 1949. The cruise ship S.S. President Cleveland, which was owned by American President Lines, shuttled between China and USA in the 1950s. It was named after one of the Presidents of the USA.

一封由马来亚寄来的信
A letter from Malaya

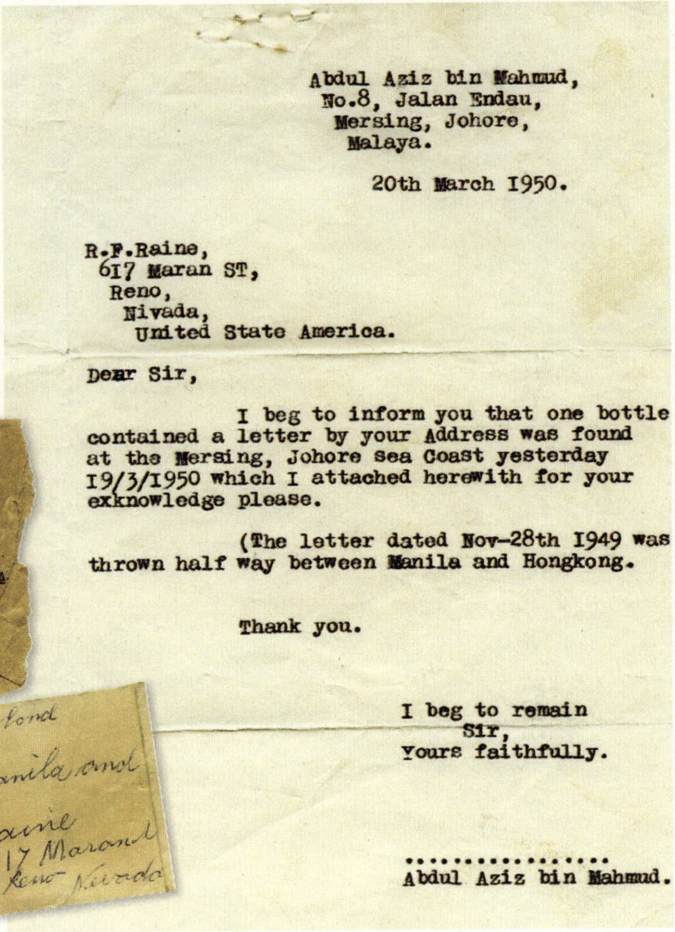

Abdul Aziz bin Mahmud,
No.8, Jalan Endau,
Mersing, Johore,
Malaya.

20th March 1950.

R.F.Raine,
617 Maran ST,
Reno,
Nivada,
United State America.

Dear Sir,

I beg to inform you that one bottle contained a letter by your Address was found at the Mersing, Johore sea Coast yesterday 19/3/1950 which I attached herewith for your exknowledge please.

(The letter dated Nov-28th 1949 was thrown half way between Manila and Hongkong.

Thank you.

I beg to remain
Sir,
Yours faithfully.

....
Abdul Aziz bin Mahmud.

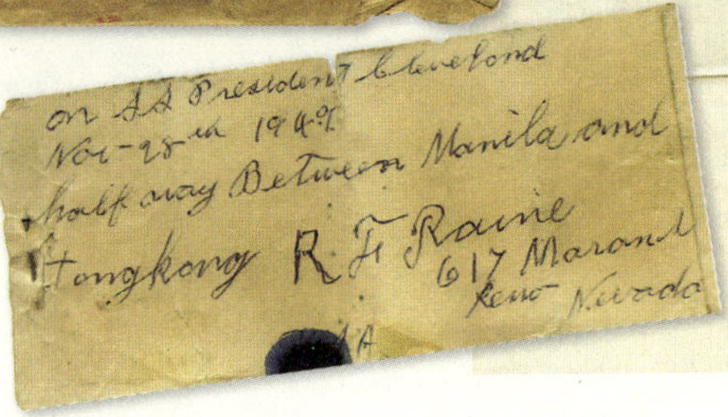

一封1950年3月20日从马来亚寄给雷恩的信，信中告知雷恩，1949年11月28日他在马尼拉至香港的半途中放置的漂流瓶，1950年3月19日在马来亚柔佛州丰盛港被发现，他放在漂流瓶中的字条也随信寄来。

A letter dated March 20th, 1950 from Malaya to Raine, which notified him that a “letter in a bottle” put into the sea by him in Nov. 1949 between Manila and Hongkong was discovered in Johore, Malay. His note in the bottle was also returned as attachment.

雷恩的圣诞贺卡

A Christmas greeting card to Raine and his family

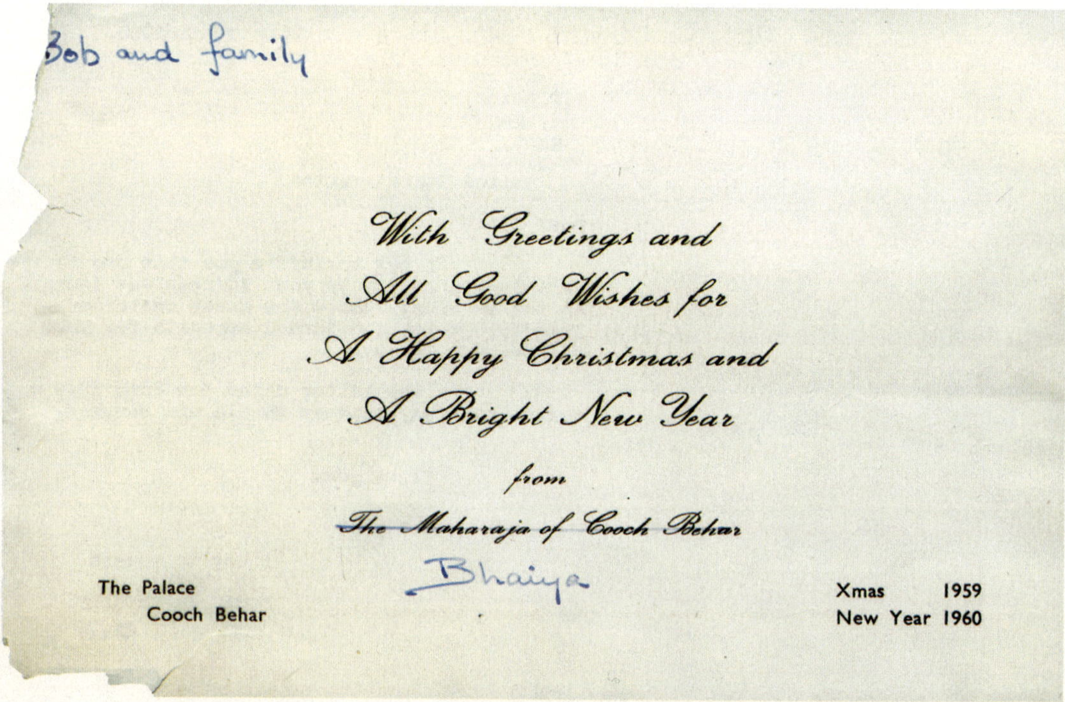

Bob and family

With Greetings and
All Good Wishes for
A Happy Christmas and
A Bright New Year
from
~~*The Maharaja of Cooch Behar*~~
Bhaiya

The Palace
Cooch Behar

Xmas 1959
New Year 1960

1959年圣诞节前夕，雷恩的友人Bhaiya自印度寄给雷恩和家人的贺卡。贺卡纸质，贺卡的正文内容如下：衷心祝愿雷恩一家圣诞节和新年快乐！背面为印度库曲比哈尔宫殿黑白照片。

Shortly before the Christmas of 1959, Raine's friend Bhaiya in India sent him and his family a Christmas card. The flip side is a photo of Bihar Palace.

飞虎将军陈纳德像
Statue of Claire Lee Chennault

飞虎将军陈纳德像，上有4位飞虎队老兵聚会时留下的铅笔签名，分别埃里克·希林、R.T.史密斯、迪克·罗西、鲍勃·雷恩4位。其中埃里克·希林、鲍勃·雷恩属志愿队第3中队，R.T.史密斯属志愿队第2中队，迪克·罗西属志愿队第1中队。

Portrai of Claire Lee Chennault, with four pencil autographs by 4 Flying Tigers veterans in their reunion. Eric Shilling and Bob Raine belonged to the 3rd squadron, R.T. Smith belonged to the 2nd squadron, and Dick Rossi belonged to the 1st squadron of the AVG.

罗伯特·赫德曼是美国二战时期第一位王牌飞行员（王牌飞行员是指打落5架或以上敌机的飞行员），他隶属美国志愿队第3中队，即“地狱天使”队，和雷恩为同一中队的战友。在1941年12月23日仰光保卫战中，赫德曼在战机座舱罩被击碎的情况下，击落4架敌机，并冲入日军轰炸机编队开火击落领队日机，更不可思议的是，这些壮举是在短短十几分钟内完成的。战后赫德曼和雷恩一同加入美国飞虎航空运公司。赫德曼一生钟爱飞行，78岁辞世。

Robert Hedman was the first ace pilot of USAAF during WWII. He served in the AVG 3rd Pursuit Squadron, nicknamed "Hell's Angels", in which Raine was his comrade-in-arms. On December 23rd, 1941, during the defensive of Rangoon, he brought down 4 Japanese fighters when his cockpit canopy was seriously damaged. He also brought down the leading aircraft in the Japanese bomber formation. Even more incredible, he accomplished the feat in approximately a quarter of an hour. After the war, Hedman and Raine joined the Flying Tiger Line. Hedman was a keen aviator and passed away at the age of 78.

Services set for noted flying ace

By John G. Edwards
Review-Journal

Services will be Tuesday for America's first World War II flying ace, Robert "Duke" Hedman of Las Vegas.

HEDMAN

His son, Robert Hedman II, said his father's funeral "was just meant to be" on May 30, when Memorial Day was originally observed to honor the country's war dead.

The elder Hedman died Wednesday, about two months after he fell and hit his head in a shopping center parking lot.

Hedman, 78, a member of the Flying Tigers, became the first American ace when he shot down five enemy aircraft over Rangoon, Burma, on Christmas Day 1941. Family records indicate he did this in less than 15 minutes and accomplished it in part by flying into a formation of Japanese bombers.

The Japanese pilots apparently were afraid to shoot at Hedman's tiger-toothed, P-40, because they might accidentally hit their own planes.

He had 38 confirmed kills during World War II and was the first American to win China's highest military honor, the Order of the Cloud.

Brig. Gen. Claire Chennault commanded Hedman as part of the American Volunteer Group fighting Japan before the United States entered the war and wrote the pilot's father, a banker in rural South Dakota.

"He is a first rate combat pilot and the reckless bravery of his attacks, both on strafing and bombing missions, and in aerial combat with the Japanese, are something you can well be proud of," Chennault wrote.

"The ace of the American Scalpers squadron is an unassuming, straight-forward farm boy from South Dakota who is known as 'Duke' to American fliers in Burma," the Chicago Daily News reported.

Actor John Wayne later picked up the nickname "Duke" after playing another member of the Flying Tigers in a movie, the younger Hedman said.

The elder Hedman, born Dec. 19, 1916, in Webster, S.D., was completely unlike the swaggering actor, however, said Al Harvey, a stockbroker and friend of 20 years. "He was a timid, nice guy," Harvey said.

Robert Hedman, America's first World War II ace, poses beside one of the Flying Tigers he flew as part of American Volunteer Group backing China before the U.S. joined the war. He died Wednesday in Las Vegas at 78.

The pilot had wealthy and famous friends around the world, including comedian Lou Costello. Hedman once asked Harvey to explain a securities rule to a friend from Hong Kong. Harvey later learned that H.Y. Kwong, the visitor, was one of the wealthiest men in the world.

After the war, Hedman joined other veterans of the Flying Tigers to found the Flying Tigers Airline, which later was acquired by Federal Express. During his career as a civilian pilot, Hedman flew supplies to U.S. troops in Vietnam, his son said.

Services will be from 1 to 3 p.m. Tuesday at the Christian Life Community Church, 800 Karen Ave., in the Commercial Center. The family will display some of his memorabilia. The family held private services earlier.

Besides his son, survivors include a sister, Beverly Austin of Venice, Fla.

72

A.V.G.

明洗染廠
LAUNDRY & DYE-HOUSE
乾洗織染工廠
織補西服大衣

迎“飞虎队”华裔老兵及家眷莅临

4 捐赠名录

Donors List

捐赠名录

Donors List

捐赠者姓名 Donors Name	捐赠时间 Donated Time	捐赠数量 Donation Quantity
陈香梅 Anna Chen Chennault（美国America）	2009年	13件
谭永昭 Wayne Tam（美国America）	2009年、2010年	19件
张家齐 Zhang Jiaqi（中国China）	2009年	1件
邝锐 Kuang Rui （中国China）	2009年	1件
丁学仁 Ding Xueren（中国China）	2009年	3件
陈灿培 Pedro & Pek Chan（美国America）	2010年、2011年、2012年	926件
John Shull（美国America）	2010年	2件
Bill Smith（美国America）	2010年	11件
Lt .Robert Walkinshaw（美国America）	2010年	14件
黄守仁 Gordon Wong（美国America）	2010年	29件
李庚申 Harry Lee（美国America）	2010年	1件
朱培基 Henry Sam Yuen Gee（美国America）	2010年	5件
甑崇运 Joe Loy Yung （美国America）	2010年	17件
余启迪 Mack Pong （美国America）	2010年	4件

捐赠者姓名 Donors Name	捐赠时间 Donated Time	捐赠数量 Donation Quantity
黄煜臻 James Bok Wong, PhD（美国America）	2010年	6件
陈其旺 Kay W Chin （美国America）	2010年	26件
陈亚 Al Chinn（美国America）	2010年	3件
黎玉荣 Wing Yoke Lai（美国America）	2010年	13件
黄洪荣 Wayne Wong（美国America）	2010年	2件
阮福志 Richard Goon （美国America）	2010年	1件
刘华新 Tom Wah S.Lew（美国America）	2010年	2件
林日新 Fulton Yee（美国America）	2010年	2件
黄启锐（美国America）	2010年	2件
Olgas . Greenlaw 陈纳德女秘书 female secretary of Chennault（美国America）	2011年	1件
迭戈 Diego Kusak （美国America）	2011年	1件
彭静吾、饶惠兰夫妇 Peng Jingwu&Rao Huilan（中国China）	2012年	1件
陈炳靖 Jim （香港HongKong）	2012年	3件
查理斯 . 彼得森 Charles Peterson （美国America）	2012年	1件

后记

只要人类存在，国家存在，战争就不可避免。战争带给人类的不只是灾难和仇恨，有时也会在苦难的深渊中腾升出人类本性的光辉。重温历史，半个多世纪前的中美联合抗日就曾经演绎了人类固有的友爱和善良、勇敢与正义。

抗日战争已经过去70多年，漫长的岁月淹没了许多珍贵的记忆。随着飞虎队文物的回归，烽火岁月宛如昨日重现。拂开历史的尘埃，将一切还原真实，让世人记住中美两国交往中最光辉、最值得纪念的一页，是一切热爱和平、歌颂友谊的中美人士的共同期待，更是昆明市博物馆义不容辞的责任。

为庆祝昆明市博物馆专题陈列馆——昆明飞虎队纪念馆开馆，为告慰曾在中国这片热土上战斗过的飞虎英雄们，也为使“飞虎”的历史成为昆明对外交流最珍贵的精神名片，成为中美两国人民永不相忘的友谊纪念，我馆将陆续推出馆藏飞虎队文物资料系列丛书，以资后人缅怀、纪念、学习和研究飞虎历史，谨记和发扬“飞虎精神”。

本书完全建立在历史的真实和翔实的文物图片资料基础上，每份文件，每封书信，每件物品背后都记录着一段真实的历史。

成稿之际，我们首先要感谢为我馆倾力捐赠飞虎队文物资料的陈灿培夫妇，正是他们的无私和热忱，才使得昆明飞虎纪念馆成立、陈列展览和馆藏系列丛书的出版成为可能。一并感谢的还有所有为我馆捐赠飞虎队文物的中外友人。此外，中共昆明市委、昆明市政府、昆明市文化广播电视体育局、昆明市财政局、昆明市侨联领导对我馆征集飞虎队文物资料、举办飞虎队展览所给予的支持和帮助，我们谨致上诚挚谢意。

由于编者学识和水平有限，又因此书编写时间仓促，深度挖掘、精度提炼不够，书中疏漏差错之处在所难免，敬请广大读者指正，如有不妥之处，请与我们联系。

昆明飞虎队纪念馆网址：www.kmflyingtiger.com

编　者

2012年11月

Afterword

Despite the human disaster and the suffering caused by the war, the joint effort of China and the U.S.to fight Japanese aggression more than seven decades ago, gave witness to the search for justice, and to the courage and fraternity of the two peoples.

Some memories of the War of Resistance Against Japanese Aggression over 70 years ago have been lost with the passing of time. However, the collected memorabilia of the Flying Tigers takes us back to that time of war; their reality displays the most glorious and memorable chapter in the history of the cooperation between the two nations. Such an exhibition of Flying Tiger memorabilia would be anticipated by the peace-loving people of both nations, who advocate friendship between the two countries. The Kunming Museum felt it was incumbent to make it happen.

To celebrate the opening of this Flying Tigers memorial as a featured exhibition of the Kunming Museum, to pay tribute to the heroic Flying Tigers who fought in this land, to use Flying Tiger history as a precious “spiritual name card,” to show to the foreign guests participating in the international exchange between Yunnan and other countries, and to commemorate the enduring friendship between the Chinese and the American people, Kunming Museum plans to publish a series of books on the memorabilia collected by our museum. This will provide a reference point for readers, not only to commemorate the Flying Tigers, but to enable them to study and research Flying Tigers history, and to experience the "Spirit of the Flying Tigers."

This book bases itself on the historically authentic and accurate images of the memorabilia, among which each file, letter or article can be traced back to a piece of history.

Upon publishing this book, we would like to express our sincere gratitude to Mr. and Mrs. Pedro Chan, who have donated the memorabilia of the Flying Tigers. Without their selfless and devoted effort, this memorial, the exhibition, and the books would not have become a reality. We are also indebted to those, at home and abroad, who have previously donated Flying Tigers memorabilia to our museum. Moreover it is our duty to note our thankfulness to the Kunming Municipal Government, to the Kunming Federation of Returned Overseas Chinese, and to the Kunming Municipal Administration of Culture, Broadcasting and Sports for their support and assistance in our effort in collecting memorabilia, and organizing the Flying Tiger exhibition.

Due to the editors' limited knowledge and time, and in the absence of in-depth research, it is inevitable that errors and omissions will be found in this book. Your scrutiny is appreciated; please do not hesitate to contact us in this regard.

Kunming Flying Tigers Museum: www. kmflyingtiger. com

Editor

2012.11